ISBN 978-0-656-42319-4
PIBN 10455928

ANNUAL REPORTS

of the

SELECTMEN

TOWN CLERK
TAX COLLECTOR
TOWN TREASURER
WATER COMMISSIONERS
TRUSTEES OF THE TRUST FUNDS
TRUSTEES OF THE PUBLIC LIBRARY
COMMISSIONERS OF THE LIGHTING PRECINCT

AND SCHOOL DISTRICT

OF THE

TOWN OF

ALTON

NEW HAMPSHIRE

FOR THE FISCAL YEAR ENDING DECEMBER 31st

1960

PRINTED BY KINGSWOOD PRESS, WOLFEBORO, N. H.

1960

TABLE OF CONTENTS

Fire Alarm Signals 3

Town Officers 4

Budget 7

Warrant for Town Meeting 11

Balance Sheet 18

Comparative Receipts and Expenditures 20

Summary of Payments 22

Details of Payments 23

      Police Department 26

      Fire Department 27

      Highway Department 29

Summary of Receipts 33

Treasurer's Report 36

Town Clerk's Report 38

Tax Collector's Records 38

Compilation of Trust Funds 46

Trust Fund Investments 54

Gilman Library 56

Building Inspector 57

Lighting Precinct 57

Water Department 58

Statement of Bonded Debt 59

Auditor's Report 63

Marriages 67

Births for 1960 68

Deaths 69

School District 71

School District Index 72

FIRE ALARM SIGNALS

Box No.	Location
3	Brush fire. Repeat three times
4	Alton Bay Fire Station.
5	Central Schoolhouse.
6	Town Hall.
12	Campground Store.
13	Alton Bay, near Lester Downing residence.
14	Gilman Road, corner Mitchell Avenue.
24	Main Street, corner School Street.
26	Main Street, Wolfeboro Hill.
31	Oak Birch Inn.
32	Gilmanton Road, corner Mill Street.
36	Opposite Wyman's Garage.
41	Bay Schoolhouse.
42	Main Street, foot Rollin's Hill.
43	Main Street, near Fred Colbath residence.
2-2-2	Out-of-town call. All firemen to report at station.
1-1	All-out signal.
2	Blasts at 7.30 a.m., no school all day.
2	Blasts at 11.30 a.m., no afternoon session.
2	Blasts at 7.30 p.m., Fire Department meeting.
1	Blast, water to be shut off in thirty minutes.

NOTICE

Brush fire, chimney fire, and all outside fire alarms are to be telephoned to the Alton operator, who will sound the proper alarm, and notify the proper authorities. This will be done by means of a control box now in the central office. State clearly the nature, extent and location of the fire. By complying with the above much time and property may be saved.

INSTRUCTIONS FOR OPERATING A BOX

Opening a box does not sound alarm: Pull down handle. Anyone sounding alarm to remain at box to direct firemen. Second alarm to be sounded by order of the chief engineer only. Test alarm every day at 12.45. Do not sound alarm unless necessary.

RAWLAND DORE, CHAS. T. BEAUDETTE,
WESTON ALDEN, Fire Wards of Alton.

TOWN OFFICERS

Selectmen

HARRY M. ALLEN	Term Expires 1961
CHARLES J. BEAUDETTE	Term Expires 1962
FREDERICK M. PERKINS	Term Expires 1963

Clerk	Treasurer
RALPH M. JARDINE	ELEANOR HORNE

Tax Collector
RAYMOND DUNCAN

Auditors
MADOLYN LAWRENCE   JUDSON H. DOWNING

Trustees of Trust Funds

FRANK M. AYER	Term Expires 1961
WILLARD A. WALLACE	Term Expires 1962
ARCHIE A. HORNE	Term Expires 1963

Trustees of Public Library

HAROLD CLOUGH	Term Expires 1961
AGNES THOMPSON	Term Expires 1962
DONALD GOWEN	Term Expires 1963

Precinct Commissioners
RALPH JARDINE
CHARLES H. ANDREWS   RICHARD DOWNING

Representative to the General Court
ARTHUR S. ROLLINS

Moderator
FRED PERKINS

Supervisors of the Check List
THELMA V. FOSIE   BURTON S. HALE
HILMA F. DODGE

TOWN OFFICERS

Chief of Police	**Constable**
A. DONALD STINSON	RICHARD L. CATE

Highway Agent	**Health Officer**
MERLE GASSETT	CHARLES H. ANDREWS

Fire Wards
WESTON ALDEN
HERBERT CARD   HAROLD CLOUGH

Forest Fire Warden
HAROLD E. PRIME

Deputy Forest Fire Wardens
HAROLD CLOUGH   CHARLES ROBERTS
WESTON ALDEN   HERBERT CARD
KENNETH CHASE

School Board
JUDSON DOWNING   Term Expires 1961
HERBERT D. CARD   Term Expires 1962
GLADYS E. HOWE   Term Expires 1963

Superintendent of Schools
JASON E. BOYNTON

Librarian
AGNES THOMPSON

Justice of Municipal Court
JOSEPH A. O'BRIEN

Water Commissioners
RALPH JARDINE   Term Expires 1961
LLOYD KIDDER   Term Expires 1962
HERBERT D. CARD   Term Expires 1963

Budget Committee

DOWNING JONES	Term Expires 1961
ARCHIE HORNE	Term Expires 1961
HAROLD CLOUGH	Term Expires 1961
RICHARD DOWNING	Term Expires 1962
RAY WHIPPLE	Term Expires 1962
HAROLD PRIME	Term Expires 1962
ROBERT E. JONES	Term Expires 1963
GEORGE SHAW	Term Expires 1963
OLIVER BARNES	Term Expires 1963

GLADYS E. HOWE, School Committee

HARRY M. ALLEN, Selectman

BUDGET OF THE TOWN OF ALTON N. H.

Sources of Revenue:	Estimated Revenue 1960	Actual Revenue 1960	Estimated Revenue 1961
From State:			
Interest and Dividends Tax	$ 5,000.00	$ 5,241.71	$ 5,000.00
Railroad Tax	700.00	830.19	700.03
Savings Bank Tax	75.00	46.19	0. 00
Reimbursement a/c State and Federal forest lands	14.57	14.03	14.00
For Fighting Forest Fires		49.89	
Reimbursement a/c Old Age Assistance		413.39	
Water Resources Board	100.00	135.47	100.00
From Local Sources Except Taxes:			
Dog Licenses		389.50	200.00
Business Licenses, Permits and Filing Fees	375.00	458.66	200.00
Fines and Forfeits, Municipal Court	175.00	653.25	
Rent of Town Hall and Other Bldgs	400.00	711.00	600.00
Income from Trust Funds		218.62	
Income of Departments:			
Highway, (including rental of equipment			
Motor Vehicle Permit Fees		1,026.72	
Withdrawals from Surplus uncoll'ed Taxes	9,000.00	10,836.29	10,000.00
Town Truck			3,300.00
Police Cruiser			2,500.00
Duncan Land			750.00
Blake Land at Hill's Pond			500.00
Amount Raised by Issue of Bonds or Notes:			

	Appropriations 1960	total Expenditures 1960	Appropriations 1961
School Street			17,000.00
Swimming			25,000.00
Loader and York Rake			26,000.00
Pay.Loader with Back Hoe			10,000.00
Fire Station	4,000.00	4,000.00	
Water Department	5,000.00	5,000.00	
Town Road Program	6,150.00	6,150.00	
From Local Taxes Other Than Property Taxes:			
Poll Taxes—Regular at $2	1,100.00	1,104.00	1,000.00
National Bank Stock Taxes	25.00	29.90	29.90
Yield Taxes		1,972.59	
ALL REVENUES FROM ALL SOURCES EXCEPT PROPERTY TAXES	32,114.57	39,281.40	102,933.90
AMT. TO BE RAISED BY PROPERTY TAXES			116,938.24
(Exclusive of County and School Taxes)			
TOTAL REVENUES			$219,872.14

Purposes of Expenditures:

Current Maintenance Expenses:

1 General Government:

	Appropriations 1960	total Expenditures 1960	Appropriations 1961
Town Officers' Salaries	$ 4,200.00	$ 3,957.30	$ 4,500.00
Town Officers' Expenses	3,250.00	3,164.15	3,000.00
Election and Registration Expenses	1,000.00	946.01	500.00
Municipal Court Expenses	350.00	351.25	355.00
Expenses Town Hall and Other Town Bldgs.	5,600.00	5,348.64	5,000.00
Employees' Retirement and Social Security	1,200.00	1,269.28	1,350.00

Protection of Persons and Property:

Police ...	7,150.0	7,979.48	2,500.00
Police Department	8,660.00	8,470.07	9,220.00
Fire Department	1,050.00	723.00	7,800.00
Wh Exterm.—Blister Rust & Care of Bees			800.00
Insurance	3,400.0	4,159.71	4,000
Bookkeeper	3,700.0	3,688.34	3,700.00
Damage by Dogs	100.0		100.00
Damages and Legal Expenses	3,000.00	2,735.58	1,000.00
Civil Defense	300.0	41.23	100.00

Health:

Hospital, Metro	400.0	400.00	1,000.00
Hospital, dia	400.00	400.00	500.00
Vital Statistics	35.00		35.00
Twn Dump and Garbage Removal	2,500.00	2,286.31	3,000.00

Highways and Bridges:

Twn Road Program			10,000.00
Twn Maintenance—Summer	13,000.00	12,540.69	13,000.00
Twn Maintenance—Winter	14,000.00	12,707.79	14,000.00
Steet Lig	370.00	236.70	370.00
Gnl Expenses of Highway Department	8,200.00	9,071.72	7,700.00
Resurface Church St.			2,000.00

Libraries	2,900.00	2,860.96	2,900.00

Public Welfare:

Twn Poor	2,500.00	1,127.66	2,500.00
Old Age	5,000.00	5,680.81	6,000.00

Patriotic Purposes:

Mal Day and Veterans' Associations	200.00	200.00	200.00
Aid to Soldiers and Tir ies	500.00	141.28	500.00

Recreation:

Summer and War Activities	3,700.00	3,075.00	3,900.00
Bks and Playgrounds Incl. aBd ots	5,500.00	5,185.33	4,400.00

Public Service Ent ...mises:

Fire ...tion			25,000.00
			2,000.00
			2,300.00
	1,000.00	772.41	2,000.00
	2,300.00	2,285.36	2,300.00
...An.	454.84	454.84	521.17
...25th	165.00	165.00	225.00
N. H. ...ion Guide			159.00
...ry Lakes Region An.			

Interest:

On	800.00	962.50	962.00
On	2,200.00	1,872.64	2,395.75
...y for New ...ection ...d Em. Improv.			
...s ...d Bridges:			
Tarvia	4,500.00	3,823.80	4,500.00
...n Construction—Stockbridge ...r Rd.			3,000.00
S...e Aid Construction—Town's Share—T.R.A.	1,174.92	6,514.43	1169.22
W...r Works ...tion			26,000.00
...e Land—Hill's Pond			4,000.00
New Lands—Duncan ...l			500.00
N...w Equipment—Loader with B...k Hoe			750.00
N...w ...n Truck			17,000.00
Payment on ... ...l of Debt:			3,300.00
...l Articles of 1960	23,450.00	19,881.86	
...g ...	6,500.00	6,500.00	10,000.00
...L EXPENDITURES	$144,709.76	$141,981.13	$219,872.14

KENNETH CHASE
...T E. JONES
CHARLES J. BEAUDETTE

ARCHIE A. HORNE
JUDSON H. ...WG

OLIVER W. BARNES
...D A. CLOUGH
GE...RGE L. SHAW

WARRANT ALTON N. H.

To the Inhabitants of the Town of Alton, in the County of Belknap, in said State, qualified to vote in Town affairs:

You are hereby notified to meet at the Town Hall in said Alton on Tuesday, the fourteenth day of March next, at nine o'clock in the forenoon, to act upon the following subjects:

Article 1. To choose all necessary Town Officers for the ensuing year, and to elect a Selectman for three years, one Library Trustee for three years, one Water Commissioner for three years and one Fire Ward for three years.

You are also notified to meet at the said Town Hall at seven-thirty o'clock in the afternoon on the same date to act upon the following subjects:

Art. 2. To see what sum of money the Town will vote to raise and appropriate to pay all necessary charges of the Town for the ensuing year.

Art. 3. To see if the Town will vote to raise and appropriate a sum not to exceed $10,000.00 for the purpose of rebuilding and resurfacing with Tarvia the Town gravel roads and Town streets, so called, and to authorize the Selectmen to borrow against the credit of the Town the said amount, on long term notes or bonds.

Art. 4. To see what sum of money the Town will vote to raise and appropriate for the repairs of highways and bridges for the ensuing year in addition to that required by law.

Art. 5. To see what sum of money the Town will vote to raise and appropriate for the removal of snow from the Town highways for the ensuing year.

Art. 6. To see what sum of money the Town will vote to raise and appropriate for the purchase of Tarvia and application of same.

Art. 7. To see if the Town will vote to raise and appropriate the sum of $1,169.22 provided that the State will contribute the sum of $7,794.82 for Class V. roads, so called.

Art. 8. To see if the Town will vote to authorize the Selectmen to borrow necessary monies in anticipation of taxes.

Art. 9. To see what sum of money the Town will vote to raise and appropriate for the decoration of Soldier's graves.

Art. 10. To see what sum of money the Town will vote to raise and appropriate for the maintenance of the Public Library in addition to that required by law.

Art. 11. To see if the Town will vote to raise and appropriate the sum of $521.17 to the Lakes Region Association of New Hampshire for the purpose of publicizing and promoting the natural advantages and resources of the Town.

Art. 12. To see if the Town will vote to raise and appropriate the sum of $159.00 to the New England Guide for the purpose of publicizing and promoting the natural advantages and resources of the Town.

Art. 13. To see if the Town will vote to raise and appropriate the sum of $225.00 for a special edition of the 25th anniversary of the Lakes Region Association, advertising the natural resources and advantages of the Town.

Art. 14. To see if the Town will vote to raise and appropriate the sum of $250.00 for spraying trees along the Town highways.

Art. 15. To see if the Town will vote to raise and appropriate the sum of $350.00 for the control of the Dutch Elm disease.

Art. 16. To see if the Town will vote to raise and appropriate the sum of $200.00 to be expended under State supervision, for the control of White Pine blister rust.

Art. 17. To see if the Town will vote to raise and appropriate the sum of $3,900.00 for band concerts and Summer and Winter activities.

Art. 18. To see if the Town will vote to raise and appropriate the sum of $1,000.00 for the support of the Huggins Hospital at Wolfeboro, New Hampshire.

Art. 19. To see if the Town will vote to raise and appropriate the sum of $500.00 for the support of the Laconia Hospital at Laconia, New Hampshire.

Art. 20. To see if the Town will vote to appropriate the sum of $2,500.00 for the purchase of a combination Police cruiser and ambulance and to authorize the Selectmen to take such sum from uncollected taxes.

Art. 21. To see if the Town will vote to appropriate the sum of $3,300.00 for the purchase of a new Town truck for the Highway Department and to authorize the Selectmen to take such sum from uncollected taxes.

Art. 22. To see if the Town will vote to raise and appropriate the sum of $2,300.00 as a salary for the person on duty as operator of the Fire and Police phones.

Art. 23. To see if the Town will vote to raise and appropriate the sum of $3,700.00 as a salary for the bookkeeper.

Art. 24. To see if the Town will vote to raise and appropriate a sum of money not to exceed $3,000.00 to be used for road repairs and improvements on the Stockbridge Corner road, starting at Route #28 and running easterly to the Alton-New Durham line, approximately 1½ miles, said repairs to consist of the application of Tarvia to the first mile which has already been prepared in 1960 and the remainder of this money to be used to finish widening the road where necessary.

(By petition)

Art. 25. To see if the Town will vote to raise and appropriate a sum not to exceed $4,000.00 to be used for resurfacing the River Lake road, starting at Route #11 for a distance of approximately ¼ of a mile to the property of Chester Griffin at the end of the road. Said repairs to consist of widening the road in local areas, placing gravel on the road and building culverts where needed. (By petition.)

Art. 26. To see if the Town will vote to raise and appropriate the sum of $15,000.00 for the purchase of a Fire truck for the district of Town known as West Alton. Said truck to be housed in the Fire house known as the West Alton Fire Station and to authorize the Selectmen to borrow the above sum of money against the credit of the Town on long term notes.

(By petition, not approved by Budget Committee.)

Art. 27. To see if the Town will vote to raise and appropriate the sum of $2,000.00 to resurface Church Street.

Art. 28. To see if the Town will vote to follow examples of newly established cemeteries in having markers flush with the ground, rather than standing monuments.

Art. 29.   To see if the Town will vote to appropriate the sum of $750.00 to purchase the Duncan land located at the corner of School and Church Streets and to authorize the Selectmen to take such sum from uncollected taxes.

Art. 30.   To see if the Town will vote to appropriate the sum of $500.00 for the purchase of a right of way at Hill's Pond and to authorize the Selectmen to take such sum from uncollected taxes.

Art. 31.   To see if the Town will vote to raise and appropriate the sum of $25,000.00 to construct a new Fire Station and to authorize the Selectmen to borrow said amount on the credit of the Town by long term notes or bonds. This work to be let out for bid and all work shall be done by contract.

Art. 32.   To see if the Town will vote to authorize the Selectmen to sell and dispose of the Fire Station at Alton Bay the entire proceeds to be applied toward cost of construction of new Fire Station.

Art. 33.   To see if the Town will vote to raise and appropriate the sum of $17,000.00 to purchase a new loader and backhoe and to authorize the Selectmen to borrow said amount on the credit of the Town by long term notes or bonds.

Art. 34.   To see if the Town will vote to raise and appropriate the sum of $26,000.00 to completely install a gravel packed well and construct a cement block building over new well and to furnish and install a new Layne 10 inch vertical turbine heavy duty pump directly connected to a forty horse power electric motor complete with all necessary wiring and controls, pump to pump 300 GPM of water against a dynamic head of 140 pounds; also to furnish and install all necessary valves, fittings and eight inch cast iron cement lined 150# test water main from new pump location to present water main. This work to be let out for bid and all work shall be done by contract.

Art. 35. To see if the Town will vote to abolish the Alton Lighting Precinct in accordance with the vote taken at the January 31st Precinct meeting, said action to take effect on January 1, 1962.

Art. 36. To hear the reports of agents, auditors, committees or officers here-in-before chosen and to pass any vote relating thereto.

Art. 37. To transact any other business that may legally come before said meeting.

Given under our hands and seal this twenty seventh day of February 1961.

HARRY M. ALLEN
CHARLES J. BEAUDETTE
FREDERICK M. PERKINS
Selectmen of Alton, N. H.

A true copy of Warrant attest,
HARRY M. ALLEN
CHARLES J. BEAUDETTE
FREDERICK M. PERKINS

SELECTMEN'S REPORT

SUMMARY INVENTORY OF VALUATION

Land and buildings	$4,897.835.00
Electric plants	169,828.00
House trailers	16,550.00
Stock in trade	64,500.00
Boats and launches	146,200.00
Horses	1,315.00
Cows	7,400.00
Other neat stock	410.00
Fowl	2,100.00
Gas pumps and tanks	5,670.00
Mills and machinery	5,425.00
Lumber on sticks	1,175.00
Wharves	4,900.00
Mature timber	3,400.00
Total gross valuation	$5,326,708.00
Less soldiers' exemptions	114,967.00
Net valuation	$5,211,741.00

SCHEDULE OF TOWN PROPERTY

Town Hall, land and building	$ 35,000.00
Furniture and equipment	1,500.00
Library, land and building	22,000.00
Books and equipment	2,000.00
Fire Department, land and building	6,500.00
Apparatus and equipment	11,500.00
Highway Department, tractor house, shed	2,000.00
Plows and equipment	12,500.00
Trucks	6,000.00
Grader	12,000.00

Place lot building	5,000.00
Snow fence	500.00
Gravel banks	500.00
Police Department, ambulance, equipment	650.00
Other Properties:	
William C. Levy Park	4,000.00
Public wharves	4,000.00
Bandstands	1,500.00
Public beach	6,000.00
Bath house	5,000.00
Railroad property	12,000.00
Half Moon Pond frontage	500.00
Alton Water Works	94,400.00
Total	$245,050.00

COMPARATIVE BALANCE SHEET, 1959-1960

Assets

Cash in hands of Treasurer	$19,687.01	$18,646.39
Capital Reserve:		
Municipal Imp. Fund	11,209.32	11,664.46
T.R.A. Reserve	3,092.51	
Fire Department Truck	1,590.47	1,652.63
Fire Station	1,590.47	1,652.68
Accounts Due Town:		
Highway Department	631.36	108.70
Police Department		210.60
Blue Cross	376.20	378.80
Uncollected Taxes:		
Levy of 1960		45,718.57
Levy of 1959	42,120.26	1,327.83
Previous Years	2,429.17	1,893.84
Head Taxes	995.00	960.00
Unredeemed	1,348.03	1,789.93
Total Assets	$85,069.80	$86,004.51

Excess of Liabilities over Assets —3,788.87   10,531.58
(net debt surplus)

| Total Liabilities | $81,280.93 | $96,536.09 |

Liabilities

Due State:		
Head Taxes (collected)	$ 533.00	$ 135.00
Head Taxes (uncollected)	915.00	810.00
Yield Tax 2% Debt	350.16	546.27
School District	10,000.00	15,000.00
Capital Reserve		
Municipal Imp. Fund	11,209.32	11,664.46
T.R.A.	3,092.51	
Fire Department Reserve	3,180.94	3,305.36
Unexpended and Carried Over:		
Civilian Defense	200.00	
Damages and Legal	1,000.00	
Parks and Playgrounds	1,500.00	300.00
Town Hall	1,000.00	
Summer-Winter Activities	100.00	
Coffin Brook Bridge		1,150.00
Half Moon Pond		275.00
Stockbridge Road		350.00
Long Term Notes:		
T.R.A. (Class V.)	3,000.00	
Truck No. 2	1,000.00	
Truck No. 1	4,200.00	2,700.00
Grader	12,000.00	8,000.00
Water Department	28,000.00	23,300.00
School Street and New Wharf		9,000.00
New Cemetery		20,000.00

| Total Liabilities | $81,280.93 | $96,536.09 |

COMPARATIVE STATEMENT

Of Appropriations, Credits and Expenditures of Departments, Fiscal Year Ending December 31, 1960

	Appropriation	Receipts	Available	Expenditures	Unexpended	Overdrafts
Town Officers' Salaries	$ 4,200.00		$ 4,200.00	$ 3,957.30	$ 242.70	
Town Officers' Expenses	3,250.00	$ 46.73	3,296.73	3,164.15	132.58	
Election and Registration	1,000.00		1,000.00	946.01	53.99	
Municipal Court	350.00		350.00	351.25		$ 1.25
Town Hall and Buildings	5,600.00		5,600.00	5,348.64	251.36	
Police Department	7,150.00	231.93	7,381.93	7,979.48		597.55
Fire Department	8,660.00	49.89	8,709.89	8,470.07	239.82	
Bookkeeper	3,700.00		3,700.00	3,688.34	11.66	
Moth and Blister Rust	1,050.00		1,050.00	625.00	425.00	
Insurance	3,400.00		3,400.00	4,159.71		759.71
Telephone Operator	2,300.00		2,300.00	2,285.36	14.64	
Civil Defense	300.00		300.00	41.23	258.77	
Health Department	2,500.00		2,500.00	2,286.31	213.69	
Summer Roads	13,000.00		13,000.00	12,540.69	459.31	
Winter Roads	14,000.00		14,000.00	12,707.79	1,292.21	
T. R. A.	1,174.92	7,832.80	9,007.72	6,514.43	2,493.29	
Tarvia	4,500.00	216.07	4,716.07	3,823.80	892.27	
General Expense Highway	8,200.00	687.50	8,887.50	9,071.72		184.22
School Street	4,000.00		4,000.00	3,913.07	86.93	
Stockbridge Road	2,500.00		2,500.00	2,137.83	362.17	
Coffin Bridge	1,800.00		1,800.00	643.75	1,156.25	
Street Lighting	370.00		370.00	236.70	133.30	
Library	2,900.00		2,900.00	2,860.96	39.04	

Old Age the	50.00	413.39	5,413.39	5,60.81	1,372.34	267.42
On Poor	2,500.00		2,50.00	1,127.66	
Soldier's Aid	50.00		50.00	141.28	58.72
Ml Day	200.00		200.00	200.00	
Parks ad Pls	5,50.00		5,50.00	5,185.33	314.67
Gy	1,00.00		1,00.00	772.41	227.59
Damages ad Legal	3,00.00		3,00.00	2,35.58	264.42
ing and Real	69.84		619.84	619.84	
Sal Sty	1,200.00		1,200.00	1,269.28	
Sal Ns	16,50.00		16,50.00	15,04.00	1,276.00	69.28
Interest	3,00.00		3,00.00	2,85.14	614.86
Hlf Mn the	75.00		75.00	50.00	275.00
Long Term Ns	6,50.00	7,700.00	14,200.00	14,200.00	
Gty	12,06.54		12,06.54	12,06.54	
Totals	$1 4,116.30	$17,178.31	$171,294.61	$15,971.46	$1,862.58	$1,879.43
					—1,879.43

Net nd of nations $11,583.15

SUMMARY OF PAYMENTS, 1960

Town Officers' Salaries	$ 3,957.30
Town Officers' Expenses	3,164.15
Election and Registration	946.01
Municipal Court	351.25
Town Hall and Buildings	5,348.64
Police Department	7,979.48
Fire Department	8,470.07
Bookkeeper	3,688.34
Moth and Blister Rust	625.00
Bounties	32.00
Insurance	4,159.71
Phone Operator	2,285.36
Civil Defense	41.23
Bennett's	1,179.56
Health Department	2,286.31
Shore Roads	2,037.21
Summer Roads	12,540.69
Winter Roads	12,707.79
T. R. A.	6,514.43
Tarvia	3,823.80
General Expense, Highways	9,071.72
School Street	3,913.07
Stockbridge Road	2,137.83
Bridge	643.75
Street Lighting	236.70
Library	2,860.96
Old Age Assistance	5,680.81
Town Poor	1,127.66
Soldier's Aid	141.28
Blue Cross	865.80
Memorial Day	200.00
Parks and Playgrounds	3,494.08
Water Department	4,000.00
Cemetery	772.41
Damages and Legal	2,735.58
Advertising and Regional	619.84

Taxes Bought by Town		1,178.21
Discounts and Refunds		310.51
Social Security		1,269.28
Special Articles		15,074.06
Interest		2,385.14
Lake Wall		1,691.25
Half Moon Frontage		500.00
Temporary Loans		75,000.00
Bonds and Term Notes		14,200.00
State and County		15,980.07
Precinct		3,450.00
School:		
1959-1960	$10,000.00	
1960-1961	97,560.00	
	———— 107,560.00	

Total $359,208.? ?

DETAIL OF EXPENDITURES, 1960

Town Officers' Salaries

Harry M. Allen, Selectman	$	582.00
Charles J. Beaudette, Selectman		538.61
Frederick M. Perkins, Selectman		485.00
Ralph M. Jardine, Town Clerk, fees		691.48
Raymond C. Duncan, Tax Collector		970.00
Eleanor Horne, Treasurer		339.48
Frank M. Ayer, Trustee		242.50
State of N. H., Social Security		108.23
Total expended	$	3,957.30
Appropriation		4,200.00
Unexpended	$	242.70

Town Officers' Expenses

| Farmington News, printing report | $ | 821.67 |

Edson Eastman, supplies	**35.47**
Burrough's Corp., service	6.65
N. H. Assessors' Association, dues	3.00
White Mt. Power Co., bulbs	1.20
Judson Downing, auditor	65.00
Madolyn Lawrence, auditor	70.00
Registry of Deeds, transfers, deeds	70.90
Union Telephone Co., phone bills	93.00
Wheeler & Clark, rubber stamp	2.26
Charles Rogers Co., office supplies	15.75
Arthur P. Varney, postage, box rent	65.20
Harry M. Allen, mileage, expenses	246.60
Raymond C. Duncan, postage, expenses	321.95
Ralph Jardine, postage, supplies	18.19
Brown & Saltmarsh, ledgers	65.49
Town Clerks' Association, dues	3.00
Tax Collectors' Association, dues	3.00
State of N. H., report	2.00
Charles Beaudette, mileage, expenses	474.25
Sargent Brothers, tax bills	118.05
Horne's Store, supplies	7.17
Studley's, flowers	20.00
Downing's Boat Service, gas	3.50
Burrough's Corporation, service, parts	25.00
Fred M. Perkins, mileage, expenses	295.40
Eleanor D. Horne, postage	10.00
Curtis Whittier, sign	8.50
Foster Press, printing	13.50
Willard Wallace, surveying	199.00
White Lodge, meals	11.00
Frank M. Ayer, expenses, mileage	49.70
Ethel Dodge, typing deed	4.00

Total expended	$ 3,164.15
Appropriated	3,250.00
Unexpended	$ 85.85

Election and Registration

Farmington News, checklists	$	98.00
White Lodge, meals		129.28
Ethel Witherbee, inspector		40.00
Gladys E. Howe, inspector		49.00
Elizabeth Beaudette, inspector		49.00
Doris McGrath, inspector		16.00
Charles J. Beaudette, inspector		20.00
Fred M. Perkins, moderator		115.00
Kenneth Chase, inspector		12.00
Donald Desautell, inspector		12.00
Harold Clough, inspector		12.00
Nelle S. P. Clough, supervisor		39.00
Clarence Hills, police duty		13.34
Robert Sederquist, inspector		28.00
Joseph A. Fabry, meals		44.25
Hilma Dodge, supervisor		88.00
Thelma Fosie, supervisor		64.00
Burton M. Hale, supervisor		98.00
Robert Reinholz, inspector		6.00
Richard Cate, police duty		8.00
Charles Andrews, labor, material		5.14
Total expended	$	946.01
Appropriation		1,000.00
Unexpended	$	53.99

Health Department

Ralph Drew, labor	$	478.32
Charles Lovett, labor		1,224.71
State of N. H., social security		35.98
Highway Department, labor		57.50
Herbert Card, labor, equipment		377.50
Charles Andrews, health officer		63.91
C. Whittier, signs		21.00
Clarence Hills, labor		9.89

George Wakefield Estate, gravel	17.50
Total expended	$ 2,286.31
Appropriation	2,500.00
Unexpended	$ 213.69

Police Department

Charles Plastridge, payroll, mileage	$ 2,997.31
Richard L. Cate, payroll, mileage	2,172.83
Joseph Keniston, payroll, mileage	890.78
A. Donald Stinson, payroll, mileage	260.101
Clarence Hills, payroll	214.20
Robert Boudrow, payroll	101.62
Donald C. Alden, payroll	97.70
Edwin Chamberlain, payroll	78.23
Francis Howe, payroll	46.38
Kenneth Chamberlain, payroll	38.33
William Bartlett, payroll	35.15
Arthur Laurion, payroll	32.96
Wesley Flanders, payroll	11.51
George Lamper, payroll	9.69
Charles Beaudette, payroll	5.50
Albert Barnes, payroll	5.40
Harvey Woodman, payroll	2.42
Dana Morse, payroll	2.42
Albert Newcomb, payroll	2.42
Warren Adams, payroll	1.88
State of N. H., social security	173.84
Internal Revenue, withholding tax	53.00
Union Telephone Co., phone bills	275.95
White Mt. Power, blinker lights	113.91
Leon Richardson, radio repairs	90.34
Stella Dore, used typewriter	50.00
Downing's Boat Service, gas, oil	47.93
Varney's Printing, forms	24.28
Huggins Hospital, supplies	19.39
Farmington News, printing	18.00

R. H. Smith Co., oxygen	15.10
DeMambro, battery	16.26
S. M. Spencer Co., badges	11.54
J. Jones & Son, supplies	7.59
Morrell's Store, supplies	5.58
Western Auto, light	5.35
Dr. Appleyard, blood test	5.00
Commercial Services, radio tube	3.00
Sanels Auto, supplies	2.83
McGrath's Store, laundry	2.44
Wyman's Garage, inspections	2.00
Wolfeboro Laundry, laundry	.75
Horne's Store, supplies	.35

Total expenditures	$ 7,979.48
Appropriation	7,650.00
Overexpended	$ 329.48

Library

Alton Fuel Company, fuel oil	$ 265.58
White Mt. Power Co., electric bills	74.91
Union Telephone Co., phone bills	132.47
Lester McCassey, janitor	373.50
Agnes Thompson, librarian	1,950.00
State of N. H., social security	24.00
Harold Hubscher, painting	27.50
Alden Machine Co., supplies	13.00

Total expended	$ 2,860.96
Appropriation	2,900.00
Unexpended	$ 39.04

Fire Department

Downing's Boat Service, gas, oil, repairs	$ 43.84
Wyman's Garage, gas, oil, repairs	65.41
Alden's Garage, parts, repairs	94.60

Alton Fuel Company, fuel, labor, parts	877.15
White Mt. Power Co., electric bills	128.32
Reed Oil Service, fuel	76.62
Union Telephone, phone bills	248.10
George Babb, supplies	4.10
Clifford Gilman, snow shoveling	50.05
N. E. Tel. & Tel. Co., phone bills	270.75
J. Jones & Son, supplies	6.60
Boudrow's Station, gas	1.59
Gilbert Agency, insurance	200.85
Gan's Tire Company, tires	180.00
Willey's, express	3.82
Harold Prime, fire bills	238.12
Herbert D. Card, radio	300.00
State of N. H., supplies	42.14
Norman Randlett, plans	100.00
Blanchard Associates, new equipment	1,105.88
Leon Richardson, radio repairs	49.60
Edward Gustafson, steward	77.80
Alton Bottled Gas, gas	14.50
H. Provost, dues	57.00
American Fire Equipment, new equipment	562.16
Loon Cove Shop, gas	3.40
Manchester Oxygen Co., parts	3.70
Rawland Dore, payroll	1,335.00
Alton Water Department, hydrant rentals	1,980.00
David Birdsey, steward	98.55
Charles Trickey, steward	236.25
McGrath's Store, supplies	.21
Philip Droste, expenses	13.96

Total expended	$ 8,470.07
Appropriation	8,660.00
Unexpended	$ 189.93

Town Hall and Other Buildings

Charles H. Andrews, janitor	$ 484.92

Alton Fuel Company, fuel, parts	1,583.18
White Mt. Power Co., electric bills	409.53
I. G. A. Store, janitor supplies	7.82
Union Telephone Co., phone bills	287.90
State of N. H., social security	28.75
J. Jones & Son, supplies	19.91
West Company, janitors' supplies	200.32
Bosco-Bell Company, mower	92.40
Woodlands Store, plants	3.75
Boudrow's Station, gas	1.27
Chester W. Littlefield, janitor	484.93
Richard Puleo, electrical repairs	99.35
Fred M. Perkins, labor, material	37.45
A. Cohen Company, steel beam	85.40
C. Roy Barnes, painting	860.64
Russell Jones, plumbing repairs	30.76
Robert Carr, welding	15.00
Oliver Barnes, labor, material	357.10
Highway payroll, tractor shed work	18.35
Alton Water Department, 1960 water bills	89.50
Boudrow's Electric, labor, Xmas lights	35.00
Horne's Store, supplies, Xmas lights	115.41

Total expended	$ 5,348.64
Appropriation	5,600.00
Unexpended	$ 251.36

General Expense of Highways

Robert Carr, welding	$ 110.00
Downing's, gas, oil	203.80
Hillsgrove's, gas, oil	211.89
Wyman's Garage, gas, oil, repairs	1,049.20
Alden's Garage, gas, oil, repairs	290.49
Weinstein Co., supplies	20.70
Alton Fuel Co., fuel, deisel oil	771.05
Woodland's Store, gas, oil	261.17
Scott Machine Co., grader parts	1,627.94

Panther Oil, lube oil	146.30
N. H. Explosives, supplies	211.02
Amoco Station, gas, oil	177.11
J. Jones & Son, supplies	114.63
Palmer Hardware, supplies	12.33
White Mt. Power, electricity	67.63
Prospect Lumber, planks	45.64
Boudrow's Station, gas, oil	542.95
Simpson Co., tires	137.42
Irving Roberts, welding	19.00
Lynn's Store, gas	3.39
Tilton Sand Co., cold patch	363.09
Prison Industries, culvert	254.20
Fred Hasting, tires	60.00
Sanel's, supplies	5.58
Busy Corner Store, gas	89.01
Herbert Card, saw	100.00
George Wakefield Estate, gravel	96.50
Ray Road Equipment, supplies	4.97
T. Marine Co., power saw	194.75
Aetna Engineering, supplies	3.88
Beede Oil Co., road oil	168.00
J. Croucher, Inc., tools	18.52
Alloy Industries, blades, chain	281.85
Horne's Store, supplies	3.23
C. BaRoss, Inc., grader parts	84.64
International Co., road salt	724.10
Wirthmore Store, culvert	242.74
Concord Wood Co., snow fence	193.44
Schaffer Co., oil	31.80
Faltin Co., express	35.12
E. J. Bleiler Co., parts	89.73
McGrath's Store, supplies	2.91
Total expenditures	$ 9,071.72
Appropriation	8,200.00
Overdraft	$ 871.72

Winter Roads

Payroll	$11,315.21
Wirthmore Stores, culvert	242.35
M. Gassett, mileage	275.00
Internal Revenue, withholding	572.00
State of N. H., social security	200.43
Town of Wolfeboro, equipment	70.80
Irving Roberts, equipment	32.00
Total expenditures	$12,707.79
Appropriation	14,000.00
Unexpended	$ 1,292.21

Summer Roads

Payroll	$10,536.72
H. D. Card, equipment	291.00
Frank Simonds, gravel	16.50
M. Gassett, mileage	400.00
J. Hillsgrove, truck	33.60
Internal Revenue, taxes	770.50
State of N. H., social security	388.09
Roy Barnes, supplies	45.68
H. Gilkerson, gravel	3.60
Robert Carr, welding	5.00
William Messer, truck	50.00
Total expenditures	$12,540.69
Appropriation	13,000.00
Unexpended	$ 459.31

Special Articles

Alton Bay Racing Association, appropriation $	100.00
Scott Machine Company, loader and rake	5,853.06
Alton Bay Water Ski Club, appropriation	200.00
Goodwin's, new pier	4,848.00
Alton Chamber of Commerce, information	

booth	300.00
Leon Palmer, band concerts	1,400.00
Wilburt Nutter, junior band	375.00
Atlas Company, fireworks	500.00
Frank Simonds, land	300.00
Huggin's Hospital, appropriation	400.00
Laconia Hospital, appropriation	400.00
Gladys E. Howe, Xmas party	100.00
Highway payroll, Dutch elm work	193.00
Jennie Gassett, girl scouts	50.00
Madolyn Lawrence, boy scouts	50.00
Total expended	$15,074.06
Appropriations	16,350.00
Unexpended	$ 1,275.94

Parks and Playgrounds

Town of Alton, highway department labor	$ 174.10
White Mt. Power Co., electric bills	174.86
Alton Fuel Company, fuel oil	43.62
Oliver W. Barnes, repairs	699.81
Robert Rollins, painting	180.75
William Messer, labor	1,211.05
Farmington News, advertising	4.20
J. Jones & Son, supplies	18.79
Downing's Boat, supplies	36.95
Edward Gustafson, labor	117.25
Tyler Advertising, sign	12.00
Citizen Publishing, advertising	1.60
Alton Water Works, 1960 water bills	97.66
Harold Prime, repairs	14.70
Harold Clough, post	.85
McGrath's Store, supplies	7.39
Richard Puleo, labor, material	3.50
Lake Wall, labor, material	1,691.25
Total expended	$ 5,185.33

Appropriation		5,500.00
Unexpended	$	314.67

Town Poor

Alton Fuel Company, fuel oil	$	212.46
First National Store, food orders		202.03
Strafford County, reimbursement		194.90
Frisbee Hospital, medical care		181.20
Belknap County, surplus food		41.51
Ainslee's Drug Store, medicine		45.00
Charles Beaudette, overseer		50.00
R. Pelchat, board, care		44.96
Charles Noyes, rent		45.00
White Mt. Power, electric bills		54.97
I.G.A. Store, food orders		30.00
Osgood's Pharmacy, medicine		21.63
Charles Plastridge, mileage		4.00
Total expenditures		$ 1,127.66
Appropriation		2,500.00
Unexpended		$ 1,372.34

SUMMARY OF RECEIPTS, 1960

Current year taxes:	
Property	$181,979.76
Polls	872.00
National Bank	29.90
Yield	1,182.59
Head	2,935.00
Previous years:	
Property	40,181.90
Polls	232.00
Yield	51.08
Head	790.00
Interest	1,199.18

Head tax penalties	83.50
Tax sales redeemed	866.04
From State	16,821.59
Dog licenses	389.50
Permits and filing fees	458.66
Fines and forfeits	653.25
Rent town property	711.00
Income from departments	1,412.12
Motor vehicles	10,836.29
Water department	5,579.39
Shore roads	1,600.00
Temporary loans	75,000.00
Term notes	9,000.00
Refunds	117.08
Capital reserve funds	3,138.89
Sale of town property	67.50
Bennett's barn	1,169.20
Blue Cross	900.30
Total receipts	$358,257.72
On hand January 1, 1960	19,687.01
Grand total	$377,944.73

REPORT OF DISTRICT FIRE CHIEF

Prevention Is Your Business

Carelessness, HUMAN CARELESSNESS, causes 9 out of 10 forest fires. Each year 200,000 fires burn over 30 million acres in the United States. This represents 5 percent of our nation's woodlands being wasted each year. Every fire takes its toll. Floods follow; stream flow is affected; timber, buildings, grazing and wildlife are destroyed—all because MANY are CARE-

LESS with fire in and near woodland. This can be remedied. YOU can put an end to this shameful waste! PREVENTION is YOUR business!

YOU, whether YOU be a farmer, homemaker, business or professional man or woman, municipal, state or federal official, clerk or woodsman can play an important part in the continuing and vital prevention program.

First—by setting a good example YOURSELF—being sensible and complying with the necessary laws and regulations governing the use of fire in and near woodlands.

Second—by using YOUR individual influence in your community and valued council with others in insisting and encouraging them to do likewise.

The following simple rules may be used as a guide both for YOU and for them:

1. Before burning, secure a permit from your local forest fire warden—the law requires it.

2. Be sure to properly supervise your burning — don't leave it.

3. Make certain your fire, camp or debris is DEAD OUT before leaving it.

4. Don't throw down lighted matches, cigars and cigarettes or from moving vehicles—make sure they are out—use your ash tray.

5. Don't burn at home—use your town dump and save yourself much possible difficulty, both personal and financial.

Number of local fires	1
Number of acres burned	2
Number of permits issued	143

Forest Fire Warden

ROBERT W. SMITH
District Chief

TREASURER'S REPORT

January 1, 1960 to December 31, 1960

Cash on hand, January 1, 1960		$ 19,687.01
Received from:		
Raymond C. Duncan, Tax Collector		230,402.95
Ralph M. Jardine, Town Clerk:		
Auto Permits	$10,836.29	
Dog Licenses	389.50	
		11,225.79
State of New Hampshire:		
Interest and Dividends Tax	5,241.71	
Savings Bank Tax	46.19	
TRA Refunds	6,063.15	
Railroad Tax	830.19	
Reimb. Taxes on Forest Lands	14.03	
Fire Bills Refunded	49.89	
Old Age Assistance Refunds	413.39	
Water Resources Board	135.47	
Reimb. Head Tax Expense	25.97	
White Pine Blister Rust Fund	1.60	
Reservoir Cover	4,000.00	
		16,821.59
Business Licenses and Permits:		
Beano	180.00	
Pistol	40.50	
Building	102.00	
Sign	5.00	
		327.50
Rental, Town Property:		
Victoria Pier	400.00	
Clam Bar	200.00	
Town Hall	42.00	
Community House	69.00	
		711.00
Shore Roads		1,600.00

Income from Departments:
  Highway—
    Private Work and Equipment
      Rental   985.12
    Refund, Overpayment labor   41.60
                                            1,026.72

  Police—
    Ambulance   104.00
    Town of New Durham   100.00
    Police Duty   1,173.58
                                      1,377.58

Sale of Town Property   67.50
Alton Water Works, Notes and Interest   5,579.39
Alton Municipal Court, 1960 Court Fees   653.25
Trustees of Trust Fund, Sidewalk Fund   218.62
Transfer from TRA Savings Account   3,138.89
Temporary Loans   75,000.00
Note, Swimming Wharf ($5,000.00) and
  School Street ($4,000.00)   9,000.00
Miscellaneous Receipts and Refunds:
  Blue Cross   900.30
  Reimbursement, S. S. Tax   28.75
  Public Toilet Receipts   131.16
  Toll Calls   42.88
  Refund, Town Officers' Expense   3.85
                                      1,106.94

Total Receipts for 1960 $377,944.73
Selectmen's Orders Paid, 1960 $359,298.34
Cash on hand, December 31, 1960 18,646.39
                              —$377,944.73

Respectfully submitted,

ELEANOR D. HORNE
Treasurer

REPORT OF TOWN CLERK

DOG LICENSE ACCOUNT, 1959-1960

123 males at $2.00	$ 246.00	
14 females at $5.00	70.00	
3 kennels	57.00	
2 part year	3.00	
27 penalties	13.50	
		$ 389.50

Fees collecting, 142 at 20c	$28.40	
Auto Permits, 1959-1960		$10,836.29
Less overpayment, March, July		5.74
Amount received (1,100 permits)		$10,830.55
Collection fees		550.00
		$10,280.55
Filing fees		$ 7.00

RALPH M. JARDINE
Clerk

REPORT OF TAX COLLECTOR

To the Selectmen of the Town of Alton:

Herewith is submitted the report of the Collector for the period from January 1, 1960 to December 31, 1960. It is divided into six parts that you may have a detailed and comprehensive picture of the various accounts,

namely :—·
1. Total Receipts during period from all sources.
2. Balance Sheet for Levy of 1960.
3. Balance Sheet for Levy of 1959.
4. Balance Sheet for Levies Prior to 1959.
5. Balance Sheet for State Head Taxes.
6. Summary of Tax Sales Accounts as of December 31, 1960.

PART 1

TOTAL RECEIPTS DURING FISCAL YEAR

Levy of 1960:

Property Taxes	$181,979.76	
Poll Taxes	872.00	
Bank Stock Taxes	29.90	
Timber Yield Taxes	1,182.59	
Interest Collected	2.48	
State Head Taxes and Penalties	2,939.50	
		$187,006.23

Levy of 1959:

Property Taxes	$39,854.37	
Poll Taxes	224.00	
Timber Yield Taxes	51.03	
Interest Collected	1,185.62	
State Head Taxes and Penalties	841.50	
		$ 42,156.57

Levies of Prior Years:

Property Taxes	$ 327.53	
Poll Taxes	8.00	
Interest Collected	11.08	
State Head Taxes and Penalties	27.50	
		$ 374.11

Redemption from Sales (All Years):

Property Taxes	$ 811.43	

Interest and Costs Collected   54.61

                                    $ 866.04

Total Receipts remitted to Treasurer
    during period $230,402.95

PART 2

BALANCE SHEET FOR LEVY OF 1960
Debits

Committed to Collector:
Property Taxes	$227,679.15
Less adjustment	6.08

	$227,673.07
Poll Taxes	1,142.00
Add adjustment	10.00

	$ 1,152.00
Bank Stock Taxes	29.90
Timber Yield Taxes	1,906.20

                                       $230,761.17

Added Taxes:
Property Taxes	$ 408.50
Poll Taxes	44.00

	452.50
Interest Collected	2.48

TOTAL DEBITS	$231,216.15

Credits

Remittances to Treasurer:
Property Taxes	$181,979.76
Poll Taxes	872.00
Bank Stock Taxes	29.90
Timber Yield Taxes	1,182.59

Interest Collected	2.48	
		$184,066.73

Abatements authorized:

Property Taxes	$ 1,362.85	
Poll Taxes	68.00	
		1,430.85

Uncollected, Dec. 31, 1960:

Property Taxes	$ 44,738.96	
Poll Taxes	256.00	
Timber Yield Taxes	723.61	
		45,718.57

TOTAL CREDITS	$231,216.15

PART 3

BALANCE SHEET FOR LEVY OF 1959
Debits

Uncollected, Dec. 31, 1959:

Property Taxes	$ 41,733.46	
Poll Taxes	290.00	
Timber Yield Taxes	96.80	
		$ 42,120.26

Added Taxes:

Property Taxes	$ 80.28	
Poll Taxes	24.00	
		104.28
Interest Collected		1,185.62

TOTAL DEBITS	$ 43,410.16

Credits

Remittances to Treasurer:

Property Taxes	$ 39,854.37

Poll Taxes	224.00	
Timber Yield Taxes	51.08	
Interest Collected	1,185.62	
		$ 41,315.07
Abatements authorized:		
Property Taxes	$ 723.23	
Poll Taxes	44.00	
		767.23
Uncollected, Dec. 31, 1960:		
Property Taxes	$ 1,236.14	
Poll Taxes	46.00	
Timber Yield Taxes	45.72	
		1,327.86
TOTAL CREDITS		$ 43,410.16

PART 4

BALANCE SHEET OF LEVIES PRIOR TO 1959
Debits

Uncollected, Dec. 31, 1959:		
Property Taxes	$ 1,110.48	
Poll Taxes	44.00	
Timber Yield Taxes	1,274.69	
		$ 2,429.17
Interest Collected		11.08
TOTAL DEBITS		$ 2,440.25

Credits

Remitted to Treasurer:		
Property Taxes	$ 327.53	
Poll Taxes	8.00	

Interest Collected 11.08

$ 346.61

Abatements authorized:
Property Taxes $ 163.80
Poll Taxes 36.00

199.80

Uncollected, Dec. 31, 1960:
Property Taxes $ 619.15
Yield Taxes 1,274.69

1,893.84
TOTAL CREDITS $ 2,440.25

PART 5

BALANCE SHEET OF STATE HEAD TAXES
LEVY OF 1960
Debits

Committed to Collector:
Original Warrant $ 3,700.00
Added Taxes 140.00

$ 3,840.00
Penalties Collected 4.50

TOTAL DEBITS $ 3,844.50
Credits

Remittances to Treasurer $ 2,939.50
Abatements authorized 95.00
Uncollected, Dec. 31, 1960 810.00

TOTAL CREDITS $ 3,844.50
LEVY OF 1959
Debits

Uncollected, Dec. 31, 1959 $ 915.00

Added during period	70.00	
	$	985.00
Penalties Collected		76.50
TOTAL DEBITS	$	1,061.50

Credits

Remittances to Treasurer	$	841.50
Abatements authorized		100.00
Uncollected, Dec. 31, 1960		120.00
TOTAL CREDITS	$	1,061.50

LEVIES OF PRIOR YEARS
Debits

Uncollected, Dec. 31, 1959	$	80.00
Added during period		5.00
Penalties Collected		2.50
TOTAL DEBITS	$	87.50

Credits

Remittances to Treasurer	$	27.50
Abatements authorized		30.00
Uncollected, Dec. 31, 1960		30.00
TOTAL CREDITS	$	87.50

PART 6
SUMMARY OF TAX SALES ACCOUNTS AS OF
DECEMBER 31, 1960

Debits

	1959	1958	1957	Prior	Totals
Balance of Unredeemed Tax Sales as of 12/31/59		$1,184.99	$86.91	$161.82	$1,433.72
Sold to Town during current fiscal year	1,178.41				1,178.41
Interest collected after sale	1.05	34.09	.39	13.33	48.86
Redemption Costs	2.00	2.25	.50	1.00	5.75
TOTAL DEBITS	$1,181.46	$1,221.33	$87.80	$176.15	$2,666.74

Credits

	1959	1958	1957	Prior	Totals
Remittances to Treasurer during year	$ 180.84	$ 572.46	$32.51	$80.23	$ 866.04
Abatements authorized during year	10.77				10.77
Unredeemed, as of Dec. 31, 1960	989.85	648.87	55.29	95.92	1,739.93
TOTAL CREDITS	$1,181.46	$-,221.33	$87.80	$176.15	$2,666.74

The foregoing report is correct and in order according to my best knowledge and belief and has been examined by your duly elected auditors.

Respectfully submitted,

RAYMOND C. DUNCAN
Collector

December 31, 1960.

REPORT OF THE TRUST FUNDS OF THE TOWN OF ALTON, N. H.

Date of Creation	TRUST FUNDS	Purpose of Trust Funds	How Invested	Principal Balance Beginning Year	Principal Balance End Year	Balance Beginning Year	Amount	Expended During
1901 Aug. 1	Herbert I. and Leonard Nte, Carrie B. Nte and Ida Nte	Cemetery	Common Fund	$ 250.00	$ 250.60	$106.24	$ 21.78	$ 8.
1909 Feb. 12	Sarah J. I. Evans			100.00	100.00	36.91	8.48	4.
1910 Sept. 23	Betsey J. Frohock			100.00	100.00	34.61	8.38	4.
1911 Jan. 25	Ameline R. Avry			500.00	500.00	356.66	49.46	8.
1913 Feb. 25	Ado S. French			150.00	150.00	69.71	13.31	6.
1925 June 3	James W. Durgin			100.00	10 00 0	4 00 0	8.61	4.
1932 Oct. 1	Davis & Gooding, O. E. Davis and Grace A. Gooding			100.00	100.00	40.70	8.63	4.
1911 Sept. 5	Lydia A. Runnells, Lydia A. Runnells			10 000	10 00 0	41.96	8.68	4.
1933 Feb. 1	Willis E. Glidden, Willis E. Estate			100.00	100.00	7.44	7.28	3.
1933 Feb. 1	Lafayette, Lafayette			10 00 0	100.00	22.75	7.90	3.
1933 June 1	Irad B. Gilman			10 00 0	10 00 0	3 099	8.48	4.
1933 June 1	Ida F. Nutter, Ida F.			200.00	200.00	58.18	16.34	8.
1933 June 1	James B.			200.00	200.00	91.70	17.70	8.
1934 Sept. 1	John F. Hanson, M. Elkins			100.00	100.00	44.60	8.79	4.
1935 Aug. 1	Hezekiah, Abbie H. Batchelder			100.00	100.00	38.56	8.54	4.
1936 Jan. 1	Wm Lamprey, Naham Estate			100.00	100.00	39.37	8.58	4.
1917 Dec. 17	Percy S. Jones, George W. Berry Estate			1700.00	1700.00	899.48	155.50	62.
1911 Jan. 28	George W. Berry			102.00	102.0 0	39.57	10.74	4.
1914 Nov. 14	Ellen Jones, Ellen Jones			408.0 0	408.0 0	483.48	48.08	4.

Date	Name		Cemetery / Common Fund				
1911 Aug. 21	Stephen C. Wentworth	Stephen C. Wentworth	75.00	75. 0	27.29	6.33	3
1913 Feb. 15	Jonathan H. Downing	Jonathan H. Downing	100.00	100.00	41.32	8.66	4
1914 Feb. 15	Daniel M. and John F. Perkins	Daniel M. ard John F. Perkins	80.00	80.00	29.24	6.76	3
		Daniel M. and John F. Perkins			38.47	8.54	3
1916 July 21	Andrew J. ... Chester A.	...ly	100.00	100.00			
		Marietta Twombly					
1917 May 16	Minerva B. Sanborn	Minerva B. Sanborn	5 0.00	50.00	15.85	4.12	3
1919 Dec. 31	Sarah J. ...ke	Sarah J. ...ke	40 000	400.00	235.05	37.48	8
1920 June 11	Lewis P. ...	...e Sett Rines	20 000	200.00	91.56	17.63	6
		Lewis P. Varney, George Scott Rines					
1921 June 1	Ella A. Field	Ella A. Fifield	10 000	100.00	36.03	8.44	3
1923 Apr. 1	Benjamin C. Glidden	Benjamin C. ... Glen	5 0.00	50.00	14.78	4.08	3
1924 Oct. 9	Bertha L. Jo...esn	Bertha L. Jones	15 0.00	150.00	83.64	13.86	4
1925 Jan. 1	Ann E. Peavey	Wm E. Peavey	100.00	100.00	39.92	8.58	3
1926 Oct. 25	Fannie Chandler	Effie McDuffee	( )				
			(200.00)	200.00	91.58	17.68	4
1950 Nov. 17	Fannie Chandler	Effie McDuffee	10 000	10 000	51.65	9.06	0
1927 May 16		Arthur B. Newhall	( )				
			(200.00)	200.00	95.22	17.84	4
1928 July 11	Fred M. Newhall	Arthur B. ... Bell	100.00	100.00	37.17	8.48	4
1950 Aug. 11	Fred M. ...	Laura Mooney	5 0.00	50.00	16.32	4.14	3
1928 Nov. 7	...Mooney	Albert D. Morse	100.00	100.00	38.45	8.54	3
1929 Dec. 3	John G. W. ...	...ice Coffin	10 000	100.00	37.17	8.48	3
1929 Jan. 31	Levi T. Coffin	Georgia E. ...se	10 000	100.00	36.32	8.46	3
1930 Feb. 27	...a E. Whitehouse	Amy ...	20 000	200.00	76.43	17.06	4
1930 Mar. 12	Amy ...h	Moses W. Morrell	10 000	100.00	35.74	8.42	3
1923 Aug. 1	Moses W. Morrell	Moses W. Morrell	10 00 0	100.00	35.30	8.42	3
1923 Aug. 1	Jonathan L. Blakely	Annie L. Sanborn	5 0.00	50.00	15.64	4.10	3
1923 Oct. 1	...es W. Sanborn	...la Young					
1923 Dec. 1	Aaron Young						
1924 Jan. 31	Lewis E. Avery	Lewis E. Avery	100 000	1000.00	556.57	92.46	29

Date			Name	Cemetery						
1925	Jan.	31	Dora J. Brown	Dora J. Brown	50.00	50.00	14.89	4.08	3.
1936	July	1	Herbert L. ⸱⸱⸱	Herbert L. ⸱⸱⸱	100.00	100.00	31.91	8.26	4.
1936	Oct.	3	S. E. P. ⸱⸱⸱	Ella ⸱⸱⸱	150.00	150.00	88.26	14.06	4.
1936	Apr.	21	Luella C. Bradley	Lalla C. Bradley	200.00	200.00	105.23	18.24	4.
1937	June	16	Alonzo S. Brooks	Alonzo S. Brooks	400.00	400.00	322.83	41.02	6.
1938	Feb.	1	Herbert E. Morrill	⸱⸱a E. Watts Estate	0900	50.00	14.84	4.08	3.
1938	Apr.	22	John J. ⸱⸱er	h⸱⸱ie A. Dore, Extx.	103.00	100.00	38.60	8.54	7.
1938	Aug.	25	Martha A. ⸱⸱en	Martha A. ⸱⸱en	1 0.00	100.00	40.11	8.60	4.
1939	Mar.	25	Levi B. ⸱⸱in	Myra L. ⸱⸱by	100.00	100.00	35.70	8.42	4.
1939	Aug.	9	Enoch Canney	⸱⸱ie M. Reynolds	100.00	100.00	38.64	8.54	4.
1939	Sept.	27	Lalla C. Bradley	Luella C. Bradley	200.00	200.00	145.42	19.86	0.
1939	Dec.	9	Lewis H. Lamprey	Lewis H. Lamprey	100.00	100.00	37.88	8.50	3.
1940	Jan.	8	E. D. Roberts	E. D. Roberts	100.00	100.00	43.65	8.74	4.
1919	June	10	Eben C. Sleeper	Mary J. ⸱⸱er	100.00	100.00	35.08	8.40	4.
1927	Aug.	31	William Selon	William Selon	100.00	100.00	39.24	8.58	4.
1936	Oct.	27	⸱⸱a A. Amazeen	Offin Merrow, James Merrow	50.00	50.00	14.86	4.08	3.
1943	Nov.	16	Oscar C. Ellis	Oscar C. Ellis Estate	150.00	150.00	89.03	14.08	0.
1943	Nov.	16	Oscar C. Ellis	⸱⸱ar C. Ellis	75.00	75.00	33.89	6.59	4.
1927	Dec.	27	⸱⸱e Wilson	Jesse ⸱⸱n	103.00	100.00	39.10	8.56	4.
1929	Oct.	1	Fona G. ⸱⸱ld	Fona G. Crosley	1 .00	100.00	34.31	8.36	4.
1930	Mar.	25	Ruth Hayes	Ruth Hayes	50.00	50.00	15.45	4.14	3.
1930	Sept.	1	Lovisa Shirley	Cyrus Harriman	50.00	50.00	15.45	4.14	3.
1931	May	1	Ada M. ⸱⸱an	Ada M. Gilman Heirs	1 0.00	100.00	39.00	8.58	4.
1931	Nov.	1	⸱⸱e C. Perkins	⸱⸱ge C. ⸱⸱ins	100.00	100.00	39.41	8.60	4.
1932	Dec.	15	Inez Q. Walker	Inez Q. Walker	100.00	100.00	39.74	8.62	4.
1934	Jan.	1	⸱⸱ah J. ⸱⸱lan	Sarah J. ⸱⸱in	200.00	200.00	100.34	18.06	4.
1930	May	14	Walter ⸱⸱er	Walter ⸱⸱er	100.00	100.00	38.55	8.57	4.
1930	Oct.	2	David Lamper Dora	⸱⸱a Varney	100.00	100.00	38.18	8.55	4.
1921	Dec.	31	Jesse Savage	Jesse Savage	150.00	150.00	78.06	13.68	4.

Common Fund

Date	Cemetery		Common Fund					
1921 June 1	Lizzie M. Lamper	Lizzie M. Lamper	50.00	50. 0	14.23	4.09	3
1926 Aug. 19	Seth C. Hayes	Seth C. Hayes	53.00	50.00	15.47	4.11	3
1927 May 16	Charles D. Marston	Luella Marston	50.00	50.00	15.47	4.14	3
1917 Feb. 15	William B. Jenness	William B. Jness	50.00	50.00	15.51	4.14	3
1917 Feb. 17	Giles H. Downing	les H. Downing	10 00.00	100.00	42.78	8.74	4
1917 May 14	Jonas M. Place	Jonas M. Place	10 00.00	100.00	37.34	8.51	4
1921 Feb. 15	Giles M. Hurd	Giles M. Hurd	100.00	100.00	39.35	8.60	4
1922 Feb. 1	M. D. M. McDuffee	M. D. L. McDuffee	50.00	50.00	15.23	4.13	0
1922 Mar. 1	Martha W. Coan	Martha W. Coan	100.00	100.00	38.98	8.53	3
1922 Mar. 4	Sarah A. McDuffee	Sarah A. McDuffee	100.00	100.00	39.78	8.62	4
1922 Mar. 22	Harry Morrison	Harry Morrison	100.00	100. 0	37.94	8.54	3
1950 Mar. 29	George W. Morrison	George W. Morrison, Extx.	100.00	100.00	32.34	8.31	4
1922 May 1	Carrie Hds	Carrie Hammonds	100. 0	100.00	39.31	8.60	4
1926 July 1	Amla Durgin	Amanda Durgin	100.00	100.00	38.23	3.55	4
1926 Feb. 27	Giles A. Barr	Giles A. Bar	100.00	100. 0	41.29	8.68	4
1931 Oct. 31	Lella Phillips	Lella Phlps	100.00	1 0.00	40.43	8.64	4
1931 Oct. 31	Richard Yeaton	Melissa Witham	100.00	100.00	38.11	8.54	4
1931 Sept. 1	Fred E. len	Fred E. len	100.00	100.00	42.67	8.74	3
1927 Dec. 27	Oliver J. M. Gilman	Oler J. M. Gan	500.00	500.00	223.77	44.09	4
1930 July 5	Lottie L. Rhines	Lottie L. Rhines	100.00	100.00	35.38	8.43	7
1931 Nov. 1	Emma A. Wes	Emma A. Wes	50.00	50.00	14.81	4.10	4
1919 Sept. 15	Ann Elizabeth Stowell	Ann Elizabeth Stowell	150.00	150.00	81.94	13.83	4
1926 Oct. 13	Clara M. Jones	Ella M. Jones	150.00	150.00	80.66	13.77	0
1927 Nov. 1	Man F. Hunt	Nathan F. Hunt	300.00	300.00	241.56	3 081	4
1931 Nov. 1	Harry E. Evans	Mabel M. Evans	150.00	150. 0	92.51	14.25	4
1932 May 1	Jacob Chamberlain	Jacob Chamberlain	100.00	100.00	38.61	8.57	4
1930 Nov. 26	Sewell E. Roberts	Ella Trask Roberts	100.00	100.00	38.44	8.56	4
1931 Mar. 20	Ang & Mer	Carrie A. Seward & Wm. S. Lang	200.00	200.00	64.99	16.64	6
1931 Apr. 1	Ante Chesley Price	Annette Gley Price	100.00	100.00	39.63	8.61	4

Financial ledger (rotated table). Reading across: Date, No., Name (as entered), Name (lot/beneficiary), then fund amounts.

Date	No.	Name	Name					
			Cemetery — Common Fund					
1931 May 1	1	Ha alm Young	Hannah Young	86.76	86.76	29.74	7.28	3.
1931 May 4	4	Fannie Rodgers	Fannie Rodgers	100.00	100.00	40.99	8.66	4.
1931 Dec. 1	1	Jm C. Young	John C. Young	100.00	100.00	39.59	8.61	4.
1931 Dec. 1	1	Romeyne B. Hurd	Mabel M. Brown	150.00	150.00	88.52	14.09	4.
1932 Sept. 1	1	Fred Hanson	Fred Hanson	100.00	100.00	41.63	8.69	4.
1932 Dec. 1	1	Clara B. Yorke	Clara B. Yorke	75.00	75.00	25.89	6.30	3.
1932 Dec. 2	2	affie B. Tibbetts		125.00	125.00	61.51	11.25	4.
		F. E. ard C. B. Tibbetts and J. E. Cook						
1933 Mar. 1	1	Sdar E. Davis	Oscar E. Davis	200.00	200.00	117.93	18.79	4.
1933 Aug. 1	1	Percy H. Mker	Percy H. Mer	100.00	100.00	32.22	8.31	4.
1934 Sept. 1	1	Capt. James Nte	Ida Nte	100.00	100.00	38.03	8.54	4.
1935 Sept. 6	6	My L. Kford	Mary L. Bickford	100.00	100.00	41.59	8.69	4.
1917 Dec. 17	17	Percy S. Jones	Percy S. Jones	2300.00	2300.00	1248.72	211.71	21.
1934 Sept. 19	19	Mo C. Varney	Mo C. Varney	500.00	500.00	328.89	50.09	8.
1934 Oct. 1	1	Carrie B. Carpenter	Carrie B. Carpenter	200.00	200.00	78.80	17.56	4.
1935 Apr. 16	16	Frank D. Morse	Dora E. Morse	100.00	100.00	34.20	8.54	4.
1935 June 6	6	Elbridge G. Ellis	Uge G. Ellis	100.00	100.00	39.06	8.77	4.
1935 Nv. 1	1	Mattie Hayes	Tie Hayes	200.00	200.00	118.72	17.51	4.
1945 Mr. 9	9							
1936 Jan. 1	1	Everett W. Emerson	L. Mid Emerson	100.00	100.00	34.59	8.01	4.
1957 Dec. 31	31	Wn of Alton		1000.00	1500.00	90.47	62.21	0.
		Fire Truck Fund						
1957 Dec. 31	31	Wn of Alton	Fire Station Fund	1000.00	1500.00	90.47	62.21	0.
1960 May 24	24	Charles C. Mooney	Katherine A. Gilman	100.00	100.00		3.50	3.
1960 Jan. 12	12	F. H. Wheeler	Agnes M. Thomoson	200.00	200.00		14.00	0.
1940 July 19	19	Andrew J. Brown	S. Mo Brown Estate	150.00	150.00	76.11	13.56	4.
1940 July 19	19	Frank J. Perkins	Florence Clark	100.00	100.00	38.44	8.54	4.
1940 Sept. 25	25	Edward L. Gld	Edward L. Gld	50.00	50.00	14.59	4.06	3.

Date	Name	Fund				
1941 Sept. 20	Ml E. ... My ... Ms. Paul E. ... kdy		125.00	125.00	48.21	10.69	4
1941 Dec. 6	Ms. Alma ... Gn		200.00	200.00	128.44	19.18	8
1942 Apr. 1	Amos L. ... Ms, E. W. ... et al		300.00	300.00	165.68	27.66	4
1942 Oct. 3	Emily Francis ... Mn P. Horne ... Me	Common Fund	100.00	100.00	36.81	8.46	4
1944 May 31	Willie H. ... Lizzie S. ... He		100.00	100.00	38.69	8.54	4
1944 Sept. 5	George S. Bassett ... Roscoe C.		100.00	100.00	38.45	8.54	4
1944 May 31	Aaron Varney ... Mrs. ... Me J.		150.00	150.00	77.69	13.62	4
1944 Sept. 10	Fred W. ... Ed A. Giles		150.00	150.00	79.99	13.70	4
1944 Sept. 12	Florence Crabtree ... Peterson ... Am.		200.00	200.00	137.65	19.54	4
1944 Nov. 10	Miller & Clough ... M. ard ... d S. ... Hll		150.00	150.00	75.18	13.56	8
1945 Aug. 8	... Rollins		400.00	400.00	227.26	37.16	8
1945 Aug. 8	... nd		100.00	100.00	38.64	8.54	3
1945 Aug. 8	... & Hill		150.00	150.00	70.58	13.32	8
1945 Sept. 8	... M. Lee ... F. Gordon ... M. Lee		200.00	200.00	116.15	18.68	4
1945 Apr. 19	Will ... ad Laura ... Gil ... Ar		500.00	500.00	349.28	49.10	8
1946 Feb. 20	This ... er Mrs. ... n W.		200.00	200.00	116.60	18.68	4
1946 June 11	Leslie		200.00	200.00	116.27	18.68	4
1946 July 2	Willie W. ... ns ... Carrie M. Card		150.00	150.00	99.66	14.50	4
1946 Nov. 7	Ge F. ... Blanche Lynch		200.00	200.00	115.87	18.66	4
1947 July 21	George W. Rollins ... e Foster		150.00	150.00	68.94	13.26	4
1947 Sept. 13	... A. ... Robert A. Frohock, J.		100.00	100.00	38.85	8.54	3
1947 Sept. 18	Belle H. Mooney ... Belle H. ... Me		400.00	400.00	257.52	38.38	4
1904 June 4	... e L. Palmer	Book Fund	510.00	510.00	00.00	50.65	50
1928 Feb. 27	... J. M. Gil ran	Book ... rd	2000.00	2000.00	00.00	140.00	140
1928 Feb. 14	Oliver J. M. Gil ran	Lyceum	5000.00	5000.00	3058.70	474.19	167
1936 May 2	... is E. Avery	Highway	1000.00	1000.00	543.98	91.26	218
1936 May 2	Mn F. ... Ge		5000.00	5000.00	747.20	379.23	0
1944 Dec. 29	... n of Mn	Mn Imp.	8000.00	8000.00	3209.32	455.14	0.

Year	Date	Name					
1946	St. 17	Gs L. Hll	150.00	150.00	46.17	12.39	4
1948	&. 17	Me M. Sdy ad Ms M.	20 . 0	200.00	93.95	17.82	6
1948	Nov. 1	Hs E. Br Ge H. Br	20 . 0	200	103.18	18.18	4
1948	D. 28	Bn P. Vn ad Grles L. Vn	150.00	150.00	59.51	12.92	4
1949	Je 6	Ha J. Gh Ba F. Sde He M.	150.00	150.00	56.53	12.80	4
1959	My 26	Mlo C. Crymble Hin H. Crymble	200.00	0.00	3.50	14.00	0
1959	My 7	He E. Hs He E.	200.00	0.00	3.50	14.00	0
1959	Ot. 30	He Bn J. Hl	200.00	0.00	0.00	14.00	0
1959	Nv. 24	Samuel A. Wr Me L. Walker	200.00	0.00	0.00	14.00	0
1949	Ag. 16	Gs H. Hs Gs H. Hs	200.00	0.00	135.32	19.27	4
1949	Ag. 22	vHe T. Br Irville T. Br	200.00	0.00	70.38	16.73	28
1949	&. 1	John E. ad Cat He F. Gn Gn					
1950	Nov. 17	Bn O. Bt Ge F. Gn	200.00	0.00	98.37	17.84	4
1951	Je 01	Br L. Felker He Br L. Felker	0.00	0.00	88.24	17.43	4
1950	M. 29	He J. & Ge B. Sampson He Sampson	200.00	200.00	88.24	17.43	4
1951	Jly 0	Ry H. /Ah Ry H. Vh	0100	0100	79.39	18.10	3
1952	Apr.	Gs G. Hs Gs G. Hs	0.00	0.00	46.82	8.50	4
1952	Apr.	Ba Ha He	0.00	0.00	76.13	17.09	/
1952	Apr.	Luella He ege W. bGh	100.00	0100	76.13	17.09	/
1952	Ot.	Fred H. Eg Ed H. Hg He	0100	0100	28.32	8.36	3
1952	Nov.	Gs E. Wr Ms ad Hs	130.00	130.00	31.67	8.29	4
1953	St. 21	Ha O. Br lBin P. Br	300.00	300.00	43.37	10.86	4
1944	St. 21	Bk W. Gy Bk W. Gray, Ir.	0100	0100	107.46	25.37	28
1954	My 4	N Bh & Br L. Bn He M. Durgin	0100	0100	23.45	7.95	3
1954	Jly 6	; Br H. Mr Carrie M. Miller	0.00	0.00	26.08	8.06	3
1954	Hly 6	Bn S. Morse He M. Miller	0.00	0.00	58.09	16.36	4
					58.09	16.36	4

		Cemetery	Common Fund					
4 Oct. 20	Lewis A. Proctor	Proctor Estate	200.00	200.00	53.97	16.20	4.00	66.
4 Nov. 4	Arthur J. Roberts	Arthur J. Roberts	300.00	303.00	92.12	24.74	4.00	112.
7 Dec. 15	John L. Gerrish	John G. Gerrish Estate	100.00	100.00	14.20	7.57	3.00	18.
8 Mar. 13	Albert D. Varney	Charles C. Fahey	100.00	100.00	14.20	7.57	0.00	21.
8 May 10	Samuel S hy	Mrs. Samuel Shorey	200.00	200.00	25.38	15.03	3.00	37.
	GR ND TOTALS		$55,891.76	$21,554.19	$4,412.63	$1,409.50	$24,9	

INVESTED FUNDS

December 31, 1960

Shares	Company	Cost	Bid Per Share Dec. 31, 1960
248	Bank of America	$ 7,368.88	$12,367.00
198	The Chase Manhattan Bank	10,701.73	12,497.75
69	Manufacturers Trust Co.	3,130.88	4,631.38
44	Morgan Guaranty Trust Co.	3,177.00	4,770.00
108	Chemical Corn Exchange Bank	5,222.25	6,872.00
95	The First Pennsylvania B. & T. Co.	3,826.29	4,679.75
54	Public Service Co. of N. H.	4,117.50	3,510.50
180	The United Illuminating Co.	4,630.00	4,856.00
100	New Hampshire Insurance Co.	4,117.50	5,200.00
249	The First National Bank of Boston	11,072.94	17,554.50
135	National Shawmut Bank	4,717.13	7,155.00
64	Irving Trust Co.	1,050.40	2,576.75
3	The Southern N. E. Telephone Co.	100.00	141.75
		$63,232.50	$86,811.88

TRUST FUND EXPENDITURES

Disbursements from Income

William B. Messer, care of lots	$ 743.00
Spring cleaning	35.00
Flowers and urns	21.00
Villie Grant, care Glidden Lot, West Alton	3.00
Pauline Kimball, care Kimball Lot, South Alton	8.00
Library Trustees, book fund	190.65
Town of Alton, sidewalk fund	218.62
Alton Water Works, service	27.98
Alton School District, Lyceum Fund	10.00
Club Progress Bureau, Lyceum Fund	100.00

Isle Stanley, Lyceum Fund	50.00
Farmington News, printing Lyceum Fund	7.25
First National Bank of Boston, ¼ share of stock	17.19
Irving Trust Co., for part of one share of stock	30.40
First Pennsylvania B. & T. Co., part of one share	23.63
Chas. A. Day & Co., 4 shares National Shawmut stock	217.00
The Chase Manhattan Bank, part of one share of stock	7.35
Deposited to credit of lot owners	1,843.59
	$ 3,553.66

TRUST FUND INVESTMENTS

Income for 1960

Bank of America	$ 483.60
The Chase Manhattan Bank	472.80
Manufacturers Trust Co.	165.60
Morgan Guaranty Trust Co.	193.60
Chemical Bank New York Trust Co.	259.20
The First Pennsylvania B. & T. Co.	215.25
Public Service Co. of N. H.	180.90
The United Illuminating Co.	256.50
The New Hampshire Insurance Co.	250.30
The First National Bank of Boston	749.30
National Shawmut Bank	321.60
Irving Trust Co.	101.30
The Southern N. E. Telephone Co.	6.60
	$ 3,656.55

Bank interest on the above	81.33

Total income from investments	$ 3,737.88
Withdrawn from banks for cemetery care	21.00
Withdrawn from bank for sidewalk work	148.62
From Agnes M. Thompson, care of P. H. Wheeler lot	200.00
From Katherine A. Gilman, care of Mooney lot	100.00
Balance from 1959	231.79

Total Receipts	$ 4,439.29
Less Expenditures	3,553.66

Balance on hand Dec. 31, 1960	$ 885.63

REPORT OF GILMAN LIBRARY
FINANCIAL STATEMENT

Cash on hand January 1, 1960		$ 177.02

Receipts

Town appropriation	$ 1,950.00	
Gilman and Palmer funds, interest	190.65	
Other sources	47.00	
		$ 2,187.65

Total cash accountability		$ 2,364.67

Expenditures

Books and magazines	$ 988.76	
Salary	1,000.00	
Supplies and postage	215.61	
Rebinding	63.50	
Repairs	9.00	
Helper	28.00	
		$ 2,304.87

Cash on hand December 31, 1960   59.80

Total $ 2,364.67
Analysis of cash on hand:
  Check book $ 1.38
  Cash   58.42

$ 59.80
AGNES M. THOMPSON
Librarian

BUILDING INSPECTOR'S REPORT

Permits for moving of building   1 $ 1,300.00
Permits for additions and alterations   19   20,755.00
Permits for new construction   34   115,850.00

Total permits issued   54 $137,905.00
CHARLES J. BEAUDETTE
Building Inspector

REPORT OF THE TREASURER OF THE
ALTON LIGHTING PRECINCT
December 31, 1960
Receipts

Cash on hand, January 1, 1960 $ 369.75
Received from Town of Alton,
  appropriation   3,450.00

$ 3,819.75
Payments
Paid:
White Mountain Power Company $ 3,659.92
Ralph Jardine, Commissioner   5.00

Richard S. Downing, Commissioner	5.00
Charles Andrews, Commissioner	5.00
Raymond C. Duncan, Moderator	3.00
Joseph O'Brien, Clerk	5.00
Gladys D. Duncan, Treasurer	5.00

	$3,687.92
Balance on hand, December 31, 1960	131.83
	$ 3,819.75

Respectfully submitted,
GLADYS D. DUNCAN
Treasurer

WATER DEPARTMENT
Comparative Balance Sheet, 1959-1960
ASSETS

	Dec. 31 1959	Dec. 31 1960
Cash on hand	$ 82.51	4,398.31
Accounts receivable	3,941.07	4,050.68
Due from State	4,000.00	
Total assets	$ 8,023.58	$ 8,448.99

LIABILITIES

Farmington National Bank	$28,000.00	$23,300.00
Net debt	$19,976.42	$14,851.01

WATER DEPARTMENT
Expenditures

Materials and supplies	$ 821.99
Mains	133.50
Hydrants	61.75

Services	1,835.00
Meters	57.00
Source of supply	109.16
Pumping station	609.09
Fuel for power	1,459.67
Miscellaneous labor	92.50
Adjustment	1.70
General office expense	33.00
Salaries, postage, legal	469.50
Notes and interest	5,579.39

Total expenditures	$11,263.25

Receipts

Cash on hand Jan. 1, 1960	$ 82.51
Receipts, Farmington Nat. Bank	15,579.05

Total Receipts	$15,661.56
Less Expenditures	11,263.25

Cash on hand Dec. 31, 1960	$ 4,398.31

STATEMENT OF BONDED DEBT
December 31, 1960

1. Issue of March 13, 1942, $20,000.00, 2¾% (Water).

	Annual Maturities Due	Annual Interest Due	Total Amount for Year
1961	$1,000.00	$55.00	$1,055.00
1962	1,000.00	27.50	1,027.50

2. Issue of Sept. 29, 1948, $10,000.00, 2¾% (Water).

	Annual Maturities Due	Annual Interest Due	Total Amount for Year
March 29, 1961		$55.00	

September 29, 1961	$500.00	55.00	$ 610.00
March 29, 1962		48.13	
September 29, 1962	500.00	48.13	596.26
March 29, 1963		41.25	
September 29, 1963	500.00	41.25	582.50
March 29, 1964		34.38	
September 29, 1964	500.00	34.38	568.76
March 29, 1965		27.50	
September 29, 1965	500.00	27.50	555.00
March 29, 1966		20.63	
September 29, 1966	500.00	20.63	541.26
March 29, 1967		13.75	
September 29, 1967	500.00	13.75	527.50
March 29, 1968		6.88	
September 29, 1968	500.00	6.87	513.75

3. Issue of April 22, 1949, $10,000.00, 2¾% (Water).

	Annual Maturities Due	Annual Interest Due	Total Amount for Year
Apr. 22, 1961	$500.00	$61.88	
October 22, 1961		55.00	$ 616.88
April 22, 1962	500.00	55.00	
October 22, 1962		48.13	603.13
April 22, 1963	500.00	48.13	
October 22, 1963		41.25	589.38
April 22, 1964	500.00	41.25	
October 22, 1964		34.38	575.63
April 22, 1965	500.00	34.38	
October 22, 1965		27.50	561.88
April 22, 1966	500.00	27.50	
October 22, 1966		20.63	548.13
April 22, 1967	500.00	20.63	
October 22, 1967		13.75	534.38
April 22, 1968	500.00	13.75	
October 22, 1968		6.88	520.63

| April 22, 1969 | 500.00 | 6.87 | 506.87 |

4. Issue of May 28, 1958, $16,000.00, 3½% (Grader).

	Annual Maturities Due	Annual Interest Due	Total Amount for Year
May 28, 1961	$4,000.00	$140.00	
November 28, 1961		70.00	$4,210.00
May 28, 1962	4,000.00	70.00	4,070.00

5. Issue of April 15, 1959 (Water), $14,000.00 3½%.

Date	Interest	Principal	Total for Year
May 15, 1961	$175.00		
November 15, 1961	175.00	$2,000.00	$2,350.00
May 15, 1962	140.00		
November 15, 1962	140.00	2,000.00	2,280.00
May 15, 1963	105.00		
November 15, 1963	105.00	2,000.00	2,210.00
May 15, 1964	70.00		
November 15, 1964	70.00	2,000.00	2,140.00
May 15, 1965	35.00		
November 15, 1965	35.00	2,000.00	2,070.00

6. Issue of June 24, 1959 (Truck), $4,200.00 3½%.

Date	Interest	Principal	Total for Year
June 24, 1961	$47.25	$1,500.00	
December 24, 1961	21.00		$1,568.25
June 24, 1962	21.00	1,200.00	1,221.00

7. Issue of December 23, 1959 (Water), $3,500.00 3½%.

Date	Interest	Principal	Total for Year
June 23, 1961	$49.00		
December 23, 1961	49.00	$ 700.00	$ 798.00

June 23, 1962	36.75		
December 23, 1962	36.75	700.00	**773.50**
June 23, 1963	24.50		
December 23, 1963	24.50	700.00	749.00
June 23, 1964	12.25		
December 23, 1964	12.25	700.00	724.50

TOWN OF ALTON SERIAL NOTES

8. Issue Date: August 4, 1960, $20,000.00, 3½%,
   (Cemetery)

Date	Interest Payment	Principal Payment	Total for Year
February 4, 1961	$350.00		
August 4, 1961	350.00	$2,000.00	$2,700.00
February 4, 1962	315.00		
August 4, 1962	315.00	2,000.00	2,630.00
February 4, 1963	280.00		
August 4, 1963	280.00	2,000.00	2,560.00
February 4, 1964	245.00		
August 4, 1964	245.00	2,000.00	2,490.00
February 4, 1965	210.00		
August 4, 1965	210.00	2,000.00	2,420.00
February 4, 1966	175.00		
August 4, 1966	175.00	2,000.00	2,350.00
February 4, 1967	140.00		
August 4, 1967	140.00	2,000.00	2,280.00
February 4, 1968	105.00		
August 4, 1968	105.00	2,000.00	2,210.00
February 4, 1969	70.00		
August 4, 1969	70.00	2,000.00	2,140.00
February 4, 1970	35.00		
August 4, 1970	35.00	2,000.00	2,070.00

9. Issue Date: December 28, 1969, $9,000.00, 3½%,
   (Schools and Wharf).

Date	Interest Payment	Principal Payment	Total for Year
June 28, 1961	$157.50		

December 28, 1961	157.50	$2,500.00	$2,815.00
June 28, 1962	113.75		
December 28, 1962	113.75	2,500.00	2,727.50
June 28, 1963	70.00		
December 28, 1963	70.00	2,000.00	2,140.00
June 28, 1964	35.00		
December 28, 1964	35.00	2,000.00	2,070.00
Totals	$7,401.19	$63,000.00	$70,401.19

REPORT OF AUDITORS

As your duly elected auditors, we have carefully checked the accounts of the town treasurer, tax collector, precinct treasurer, trustees of trust funds, library trustees, water department and treasurer of the lighting precinct along with the bank statements of the several departments.

According to the best of our knowledge and belief they are properly vouched and correctly cast and are a true account of the business of the town for the year ending December 31, 1960.

MADOLYN LAWRENCE
ROBERT SEDERQUIST
Auditors

February 5, 1961.

WATER WORKS REPORT

The Water Commissioners have had two test wells drilled on the land in back of hills at Levey Park. The first of these had fine sand in the bottom which was apt to retard the flow of water for a new well. The second well was drilled a little nearer the river and a very sharp gravel was found all the way to the ledge which was found to be thirty-nine feet below the surface. This eight-inch well has been tested to produce more than fifty gallons of water per minute which indicates a good supply of water available.

To develop this site as a new water well for the Water Department requires the building of a road starting between the Rest-A-While Park and the brook on the north side of the park. This would provide a nearly level access to this area for the laying of mains and for moving equipment for the work on well and well house. After completion of this work this road opens up this whole level area near the water for public use. This is the section the Boy Scouts have spent time clearing for picnics and also a lot of work was done here by the Lions Club a few years ago. This is an excellent area for picnicking and is available from the water if developed.

The development of this road, well and necessary mains to conduct this water to the reservoir has been presented to your Budget Committee and should be discussed at Town Meeting.

The repairs to the reservoir, consisting of relining the tank with sprayed-on concrete called "Gunite" and installing a roof to cover the reservoir, have been completed. This is a big improvement in the protection of our public water supply.

The system generally seems to be in good repair, with little trouble through this severe winter weather.

HERBERT D. CARD   Superintendent

REPORT OF NEW CEMETERY COMMITTEE

December 31, 1960

Received from Bond Issue		$20,000.00
Paid:		
For land purchase:		
To John Oikle	$ 1,500.00	
To Oliver Barnes	1,000.00	
To Clarence Wasson	250.00	
Registering Deeds	7.70	
August		
25 Elwin Hodgins, Engineer	400.00	
September		
24 Advertising for contracts:		
Rochester Courier	16.80	
Carroll Co. Independent	7.00	
Citizens Publishing Co.	52.80	
July		
25 Telephones, etc., Oliver Barnes	31.50	
October		
22 A. D. Ingells, grading	8,900.00	
23 Elwin Hodgins, Engineer	170.00	
November		
4 Fence, Chas. LePlante	1,000.00	
16 Fence, Chas. LePlante	2,076.50	
16 Advertising for wall contract,		
Farmington news	17.85	
16 Moving stonewall at back,		
Oliver Barnes	50.88	
December		
31 Balance	4,518.97	
	$20,000.00	$20,000.00

1961
January

Spring work contracted for
building stonewall at front $ 3,661.82

Water supply and incidentals   857.15

$ 4,518.97

New Cemetery Committee
By GLADYS A. BROWN
Secretary and Treasurer

REPORT OF FIRE DEPARTMENT

The Fire Department had a very good year with few FIRES. The damp weather and fine cooperation of the public made this possible. We had two calls for Forest Fires, the worst of which was in December.

After buying the essential equipment for the department and paying the expenses, we were able to end the year with a favorable balance. The branch of the Alton Fire Department at West Alton have done their usual fine job and were successful in keeping fire losses low in that area.

Your Fire Wards, with the assistance and cooperation of Morrell's Insurance Agency, conducted a successful drill and training program at our school. We had fine instructional materials and awards for this donated by Morrell's.

Our MAXIM fire truck is thirty years old and very feeble. Our so-called NEW truck was purchased in 1948 and is now thirteen years old. Your Fire Wards are asking this year for a new pumper-tanker FIRE TRUCK to replace the Maxim. Our equipment is generally in good condition considering its age.

WESTON ALDEN
Fire Chief

DECEMBER 31, 1960

Date of Marriage	Place of Marriage	Name and Surname of Groom and Bride	Place of Each at Time of Marriage	Age	Occupation of Groom and Bride	By Whom Married
Jan. 16	Alton	Wy. D. Flanders	Aon	17	Student	H. B. Lang, J. P.
		Jule D. oGeil	Alton	17	Soler	Alton
Apr. 30	Laconia	Kein C. rhey	Alton	51	rfk Driver	Rev. L. H. Moulton
		Mie A. uMg	Alton	44	tber	tia
May 21	dh	John F. May	New Durham	20	Draftsman	Rev. W. D. Swaffield
		Nancy E. Glidden	Ash	20	Inspector	Alton
July 2	Enfield	Ed C. Miller	Alton	23	Ter	Rev. W. L. Shafer
		Beverly J. Gld	Enfield	20	Secretary	Enfield
July 9	Wolfeboro	Nw J. Flaherty	Aton	42	Teacher	Rev. E. W. Wil
		Id H. White	Wolfeboro	43	Ter	Wo
July 31	Plymouth	William Willand	Wolfeboro	20	Laborer	Rev. R. S. Walker
		Janice G. field	dh	19	At home	Grafton
Aug. 6	North Barnstead	Loran E. Smith	New Durham	24	Truck Driver	Rev. W. H. ghy
		My J. Pearson	Abn	22	At rhe	North Barnstead
Aug. 13	Mer	Herbert T. Wn	Aon	28	Mt	Rev. J. J. Foley
		Paulette I. det	Ma.	24	Ter	Mer
Aug. 27	Alton	William R. Waterman	Alton	30	Wan	H. J. My, J. P.
		Bor M. ampef.	Alton	20	At rhe	Alton
A. 3	Hon	Warren F. Hs	Attleboro, Ma.	39	Tn	F. M. Ayer, J. P.
		eBa M. Ma	dMo, Ma.	29	dgent	Alton
A. 17	Alton	Dexter A. Ene	Alton	20	Salesman	Rev. W. D. Swaffield
		Linda L. Mld	Ash	19	bler	Alton
Sept. 24	Alton	Warren L. Ads, Jr.	Hon	18	aMic	Rev. W. D., a Gld
		Adis G. Hps	Ash	18	Student	Aton
Oct. 1	Gh	George T. Garland	Bartlett	31	Lumberman	Rev. R. L. Luck
		Dorothy M. Bickford	Adn	20	At home	Gdn, Bartlett
Oct. 22	Alton	Mer A. Ryan	Derry	26	dMe Setter	H. B. aBg, J. P.
		Shirley L. Waterman	New Durham		At rhe	Alton
Nv. 12	Aton	William M. v tSm	Hollis		Laborer	F. M. Ayer, J. P.
		Martha L. Porusta	Nashua		fMe Worker	Alton
Nv. 19	Ah	David A. Me	Somerville, Ma.		Shipper	Rev. C. L. Smith
		Na M. Straw	Somerville, Ma.			Adn

Date of Birth	Place of Birth	Name of Child	No. of Child	Name of Father	Name of Mother	Occupation of Father
Feb. 5	Rochester	Valerie ... Edith	4	Robert S. Varney	Elizabeth C. Drew	Electrical ...
Mar. 9	Laconia	Paul David	2	Peter J. ...	Ida E. ...	Mechanic
Apr. 12	Wolfeboro	Mary Edith	6	Charles W. Garnache	Nancy L. ...	Driver
Apr. 30	Wolfeboro	Brian Leroy	1	Edwin L. ...	Virginia M. Ries	...
May 14	Laconia	Mary Belle	2	Richard G. Frohock	Betty A. Pike	...
June 3	Rochester	Cheryl Sue	3	Donald C. ...	Dorothy C. ...	Lathe ...
June 8	Wolfeboro	Elmer ... Jr.	1	Elmer J. ..., Sr.	Patricia A. Rightmire	Linesman
June 11	Wolfeboro	... Edward	5	Alfred J. L. Richardson	Gladys M. Libby	Painter
July 19	Wolfeboro	Baby Arlene	5	Raymond E. Dockham	Arlene R. Anthony	...
July 24	Wolfeboro	... Lee	1	Wesley D. Flanders	Jaqueline D. ...	Service
July 30	Wolfeboro	Arthur Robert	5	Orrin R. Brown	Ester M. ...	...
Aug. 6	Wolfeboro	Ruth Louise	1	Richard M. ...	Marjorie L. Bradshaw	Teacher
Sept 24	Wolfeboro	John ...	1	Charles P. ..., Jr.	Beverly A. Daniels	Machinist
Oct. 10	Rochester	Erwin Harold	3	Edwin H. Gilman	Edith G. Perkins	Laborer
Oct. 16	Wolfeboro	Kevin ...	1	William R. ...	...	...
Nov. 11	Wolfeboro	Franklin Jones Jr.	3	Franklin J. Varney, Sr.	Ellen M. Elliott	Garage Attendant
Nov. 21	Laconia	Joyce Evelyn	4	Arleigh S. ...	Ellen D. ...	...
Dec. 5	Wolfeboro	John ...	3	Ralph H. ...	Virginia M. Hopkinson	Laborer

DEATHS REGISTERED IN THE TOWN OF ALTON, N. H., FOR THE YEAR ENDING DECEMBER 31, 1960

Date of Death	Death Place of	Name and Surname of Deceased		Name of Father	Maiden Name of Mother	Cause of Death
Jan. 19	Ctr. Harbor	James I. Scruton	85	James Scruton	Sarah E. Hall	Arteriosclerotic Heart Disease
Feb. 12	Rochester	Daisy G. Hurd	80	James T. Nathans	Ida M. Osgood	Myocardial Insufficiency
Feb. 18	Laconia	Anthony Tarricone	55	Frank Tarricone	Unknown	Acute Pulmonary Emboli
Apr. 3	Wolfeboro	Margaret C. Wyman	57	James J. Higgins	Margaret T. Daly	Met. Carcinoma
Apr. 8	Wolfeboro	George N. Helie	65	Joseph Helie	Madeleine Forgue	Arteriosclerotic Heart Disease
May 24	Alton	Nelle S. P. Clough	79	George W. Place	Ida F. Sanders	Cerebral Hemorrhage
June 19	Alton Bay	Baron A. Chester	48	Clifford Chester	Florence Deoss	Coronary Heart Disease
June 26	Alton	John R. Percy	23	G. Cleveland Percy	Mary Highland	Mul. Compound Frac. of Skull
July 6	Portsmouth	Clyde R. Morrill	63	Herbert E. Morrill	Martha Shannon	Coronary Occlusion
July 19	Wolfeboro	Arlene Dockham	—	Raymond E. Dockham	Arlene Anthony	Pulmonary Atelectasis
Aug. 7	Wolfeboro	Edith A. Lamont	78	Gustavison	Unknown	Carcinoma of Stomach
Aug. 20	Wolfeboro	Caroline Hassler	86	Charles Restle	Caroline Mever	Nephrosclerosis and Uremia
Sept. 4	Union	Leon L. Palmer	57	George L. Palmer	Daisy Smith	Coronary Thrombosis
Sept. 20	Exeter	Katherine A. Gilman	79	George S. Gilman	Clara Mooney	Cerebral Hemorrhage
Oct. 8	Wolfeboro	Edward H. Downing	68	Fred H. Downing	Minnie Larr	Rupture of Anuerysm of Ventricle
Nov. 5	Rochester	Erwin H. Gilman, Jr.	—	Erwin H. Gilman, Sr.	Edith G. Perkins	Bronchopneumonia
Nov. 11	Wolfeboro	Hazel A. Renna	64	James C. Wilson	Anna I. Austin	Carcinoma of Cervix
Dec. 4	Wolfeboro	May Boullier	87	James Dauphinee	Matilda Bounker	Cerebrothrombosis
Dec. 9	Concord	Susan A. Shattuck	96	Harry Shattuck	Sabra Welch	Terminal Bronchopneumonia
Dec. 31	Wolfeboro	Colin D. Blakeney	61	Garland Boutlier	Margaret Mitchell	Coronary Thrombosis

REPORT

OF THE

SCHOOL DISTRICT

OF

ALTON

NEW HAMPSHIRE

1959 - 1960

INDEX

I ADMINISTRATION

    A. Officers of the School District 73

    B. Report of the Superintendent 74

II INSTRUCTION

    A. Pupil Enrollment 79

    B. Census 80

    C. Teacher Roster 81

III FINANCE

    A. Report of School District Treasurer ... 82

    B. Financial Report 83

    C. Balance Sheet 85

    D. Salary of Superintendent 86

    E. Budget 87

    F. School Lunch Program 90

IV REPORTS

    A. Report of the Principal 91

    B. Annual School Health Service Report ... 93

V WARRANT for Annual Town Meeting 95

VI SCHOOL CALENDAR for 1961-1962 97

I ADMINISTRATION

OFFICERS OF THE SCHOOL DISTRICT

Moderator
FREDERICK PERKINS

Clerk
ELIZABETH BEAUDETTE

School Board

JUDSON DOWNING, Chairman	Term Expires 1961
HERBERT D. CARD	Term Expires 1962
GLADYS E. HOWE	Term Expires 1963

Treasurer
BEATRICE E. H. GOWEN

Auditors
CHARLES BEAUDETTE   STANLEY SANBORN

Truant Officer
CHARLES BEAUDETTE

Census Taker
GLADYS E. HOWE

School Nurse
JEANNE C. PERKINS, R.N.

Superintendent of Schools
JASON E. BOYNTON

Secretary   Asst. to Superintendent
JEAN M. WHITING   WILLIAM C. HOBBS

SUPERINTENDENT JASON E. BOYNTON'S
REPORT

To the School Board and the Citizens of the Alton
   School District:
   I respectfully submit my fourth report as your Su-
perintendent of Schools.

STAFF

"The teacher, whether mother, priest, or school-
master, is the real maker of history." H. G. Wells

The quality of instruction within a school depends
more on the competency of the staff than on any other
single factor. Teaching requires proficient individual
performance, but it also depends on leadership and
"team effort." The "team effort" is strengthened when
proficient teachers continue to work together from one
year to the next under effective leadership. Although
we have increased salaries from year to year, we continue to be in competition with larger schools and there
is a very real scarcity of competent teachers in certain
subject matter areas.

Mr. Roland Miller, instructor of commercial subjects,
left to accept a position in Massachusetts and was replaced by Miss Corrine Crowe, a resident of Lebanon,
New Hampshire, and a graduate of Plymouth Teachers'
College.

Mrs. Dieudonne Daubney left to accompany her hus-
band who resigned from Pittsfield High School Faculty
to accept a position in New York. Mrs. Thomas Thurs-
ton who had been successfully teaching in Goffstown
replaced Mrs. Daubney. Mrs. Wayne Shipman chose
not to continue full-time teaching and was replaced
by Mrs. Avon Milliner, a graduate of the University of
Maine and a resident of Wolfeboro.

Miss Patricia Cromwell resigned to accept a position in a larger school system in this state and was replaced by Mr. Sheldon Stick, a graduate of Northeastern University.

Changes in teacher assignments were made with high school teachers also giving instruction in grades seven and eight. Mrs. Matthew Flaherty resigned and Mr. Norman Houle, a recent graduate of St. Anslem's College, joined the faculty.

SPECIAL CLASS INSTITUTED IN SUPERVISORY UNION NO. 49

"The whole people must take upon themselves the education of the whole people and be willing to bear the expense of it." John Adams

The 1960-1961 school year marks the institution of a special class at the South Wolfeboro School. This school was closed for public instruction in 1947 and has been leased to the Veterans of Foreign Wars as a Post Home since 1948. Arrangements were made with the officers of Memorial Post No. 8836 whereby the building could be used for school purposes, and seventeen pupils were enrolled on September 7, 1960.

The assignment of pupils to this special class followed the administration of special tests, intensive study of each pupil's educational record, teacher consultations, and parent conferences. The pupils selected are being provided instruction according to their ability and level of achievement. This type of instruction could not be provided in regular classrooms without taking a disproportionate amount of time from the regular course of study.

Mrs. Alma Gray teaches this class of exceptional pupils. She has a rich background of training and experience in special education. The pupils are residents of six different communities, namely: Alton, Barnstead,

New Durham, Moultonboro, Tuftonboro, and Wolfeboro. Pupils from towns other than Wolfeboro attend on a tuition basis with each school district paying its proportionate share of the costs except transportation. The cost of transportation is met by the parents of the children and by money raised in behalf of these youngsters in the several towns. In Barnstead the Earl B. Clark Post No. 42, American Legion, raised a substantial sum as did the American Legion Auxiliary in Alton.

The sum of two thousand dollars was provided by the Huntley N. Spaulding Charitable Trust to institute this special class. This sum of money was needed to initially negotiate transportation contracts and to provide the necessary equipment and supplies.

One classroom at South Wolfeboro has been redecorated, the ceiling repaired and painted, one side of the roof shingled, toilet facilities improved, and much carpentry work has been completed. Although the outside of the building needs painting and there are improvements to be made from year to year, we do have a safe, warm, and attractive classroom which is being utilized to good advantage.

A CONCERN FOR QUALITY EDUCATION

"The Good Education of youth has been esteemed by wise men in all ages as the surest foundation of the happiness both of private families and of commonwealths." Benjamin Franklin

Dr. James B. Conant's booklet, "Education in the Junior High School Years" has received nationwide attention as did his first report, "The American High School Today."

I have studied Dr. Conant's report. Of course, we do not compare in size with what he considers desirable, but we have many of the specifics to a point of detail. For example, we include in the instructional program the academic subjects—English, Social Studies, Mathematics, and Science. The time allocated to each of these subjects conforms to the specifics recommended by Dr. Conant.

We are using telecast to provide Conversational French in the fourth and fifth grades. This is admittedly on an experimental basis, but reports indicate the children are making considerable progress. We are providing instruction in French to seventh and eighth grades. We do continue instruction in the basic skills with special emphasis on Reading and Arithmetic through grade eight, and such is strongly recommended by the report. Larger schools have a greater diversification of activities than we have, but we have enough considering our enrollment. In fact, too many activities in a small school can lessen the effectiveness of the academic program.

We have Departmentalization in grades seven and eight. We hope next year to have one teacher assigned to social studies and language arts, which is what Dr. Conant means by "Block-time." In this way, a teacher's special strengths may be utilized and she can correlate the work to the benefit of pupils. Also, the teacher can know her pupils better, which is an important aspect of the learning situation. The remaining subjects, namely: Mathematics, Science, Music, Home Economics for girls, Industrial Arts for boys, and Physical Education are departmentalized. Dr. Conant's recommendations in this regard are provided below:

"Block-time and Departmentalization: Provisions should be made to assure a smooth transition for the young adolescent from the elementary school to the secondary school. The following subjects should be required of all pupils in grades seven and eight: English (including heavy emphasis on Reading Skills and Composition), Social Studies (including emphasis on History and Geography), Mathematics and Science.

"In addition, all pupils should receive instruction in Art, Music, and Physical Education. All girls should receive instruction in Home Economics and all boys instruction in Industrial Arts."

The instances where Alton doesn't measure up to Conant's report are ones where a large student body is required. For example, we do not have a full-time guidance person, however, we do systematically attend to guidance in accordance with "Guidance Practices"—a booklet which has been developed by administrators of all six school districts within Supervisory Union No. 49.

In summary, we are small in terms of enrollment, but we are trying to overcome this handicap. We are complying with many of Dr. Conant's recommendations. In time, some form of consolidation may take place. Until then, we must continue to strengthen present practices so that the best possible educational opportunity is available to the youth of Alton.

THE SCHOOL WITHIN THE COMMUNITY

"What the Best and Wisest parent wants for his own child, that must the community want for all its children."   John Dewey

Much has been written concerning School-Community relationship, and it is indeed of importance. I think it is logical to consider the School-Community relationship as much the same as the Parent-Teacher relationship. For example, a pupil benefits when his parents and his teacher show respect and confidence one for the other.

Education in general is improved when a community values the education of youth and school people demonstrate their concern for the welfare of the total community. I think we have a good working relationship, and I hope we can maintain and improve this relationship as we work cooperatively together to provide a quality education for the youth of Alton.

In school business, as in all endeavors, there is room for improvement. I welcome suggestions and pledge my best efforts to serve the Alton School District effectively as Superintendent of Schools.

I sincerely appreciate the cooperation extended me by the School Board, Principal Flaherty, Teachers, Custodian, Bus Drivers and Citizens of Alton.

Respectfully submitted,

JASON E. BOYNTON
Superintendent of Schools

JEB/jah

II INSTRUCTION

A. PUPIL ENROLLMENT
September, 1960

CENTRAL SCHOOL

Grade	Total	Resident	Tuition
7	35	26	9
8	29	23	6
9	28	23	5
10	23	17	6
11	5	1	4
12	14	12	2
	134	102	32

MEMORIAL SCHOOL

Grade	Total	Resident	Tuition
1	22	22	
2	25	24	1
3	21	21	
4	18	18	
5	27	18	9
6	27	22	5
	140	125	15

B.   CENSUS
September 30, 1960

Total number of boys and girls living in Alton on September 1, from birth through the age of 18 years:

1960	380
1959	399
1958	403
1957	385
1956	371
1955	331
1954	318
1953	330
1952	326
1951	295

C. TEACHER ROSTER, 1960 - 1961

CENTRAL SCHOOL

Name	Assignment	Years Experience	Degree
Matthew J. Flaherty	Principal; Biology, General Business	19	B.S., M.Ed.
Mrs. Paulette I. Alden	Arithmetic, Grades 7 and 8	3	B.A.
John L. Bucher	English, I, II, III, IV, Grade 8	17	B.Ed.
Miss Corrine A. Crowe	Commercial	0	B.Ed.
Mrs. Eleanor J. Hayes	Home Economics, Social Studies, Grade 7	29	B.Ed.
Norman E. Houle	Mathematics and Science	0	B.A.
Donald F. Jacques	Social Studies, Grades 8 and 9	1	B.Ed.
Mrs. Laura G. Miles	French, I, II, III, Grades 7 and 8	5	B.A.
Raymond J. Plante	Industrial Arts, Physical Education	2	B.Ed.

MEMORIAL SCHOOL

Name	Assignment	Years Experience	Degree
Mrs. Elizabeth M. Parker	Principal, Grade 5	41	Diploma
Mrs. Eugenia D. Hutchins	Grade 2	14	B.Ed.
Mrs. Frances H. Miliner	Grade 4	0	B.A.
Wilbur Nutter	Band and Chorus	35	
Sheldon Stick	Grade 6	0	B.A.
Mrs. Simone Thurston	Grade 3	1	B.Ed.
Miss Genevieve Webber	Grade 1	3	B.A.

III FINANCE

A. REPORT OF SCHOOL DISTRICT TREASURER
For the Fiscal Year July 1, 1959 to June 30, 1960

SUMMARY

Cash on Hand July 1, 1959		$ 96.41
Received from Selectmen:		
Current Appropriation	$106,397.88	
Received from State Treasurer:		
State Funds	2,700.00	
Federal Funds	1,748.38	
Received from Tuitions	14,616.39	
Received from all Other Sources	2,008.22	
Total Receipts		$127,470.87
Total Amount Available for Fiscal Year		$127,567.28
Less School Board Orders Paid		127,314.31
Balance on Hand June 30, 1960		$ 252.97

BEATRICE E. H. GOWEN
District Treasurer

July 12, 1960.

AUDITORS' CERTIFICATE

This is to certify that we have examined the books, vouchers, bank statements and other financial records of the treasurer of the school district of Alton, N. H., of which the above is a true summary for the fiscal year ending June 30, 1960 and find them correct in all respects.

CHARLES J. BEAUDETTE
STANLEY G. SANBORN
Auditors

July 21, 1960.

B. FINANCIAL REPORT

Receipts

Federal Aid:

Smith-Hughes and George Barden	$ 167.65	
National School Lunch and Special Milk	862.90	
Other, P.L. 864	717.83	
Total		$ 1,748.38

State Aid:

Building Aid	2,700.00

Local Taxation:

Current Appropriation	106,397.88

Other Sources:

Elementary School Tuitions	$ 7,689.53	
Secondary School Tuitions	6,674.86	
Notes or Bonds	45,000.00	
Other	266.00	
Total		59,630.39

Total Net Receipts from All Sources	$170,476.65

Cash on Hand, July 1, 1959:

General Fund	$ 96.41	
Capital Outlay Fund	16.30	
Total		112.71

Grand Total Net Receipts	$170,589.36

Payments

Administration:

Salaries of District Officers	$ 464.00
Superintendent's Salary	1,138.50
Tax for State Wide Supervision	530.00
Salaries of Other Administrative Personnel	1,592.66

Supplies and Expenses	1,050.39
Instruction:	
Teachers' Salaries	54,626.76
Principals' Salaries	5,900.00
Books and Other Instructional Aids	1,282.32
Scholars' Supplies	3,740.52
Supplies and Other Expenses	1,106.31
Operation of School Plant:	
Salaries of Custodians	6,260.48
Fuel or Heat	4,095.07
Water, Light, Supplies and Expenses	2,894.40
Maintenance of School Plant:	
Repairs and Replacements	1,507.36
Auxiliary Activities:	
Health Supervision	1,485.48
Transportation	12,573.70
Special Activities and Special Funds	1,007.14
School Lunch	1,143.00
Fixed Charges:	
Retirement	4,359.94
Insurance, Treas. Bonds and Expenses	1,295.14
Total Net Current Expenses	$108,053.17
Capital Outlay:	
Additions and Improvements to Buildings	34,333.85
New Equipment	6,472.54
Debt and Interest:	
Principal of Debt	9,000.00
Interest on Debt	3,927.24
Total Net Payments for all Purposes	$161,786.80

Cash on Hand at End of Year, June 30, 1960:

General Fund	252.97
Capital Outlay Fund	8,549.59

Grand Total Net Payments	$170,589.36

C. BALANCE SHEET, JUNE 30, 1960

ASSETS

Cash on Hand June 30, 1960	$ 8,802.56	
Accounts Due to District:		
From State NDEA	234.53	
Total Assets		$ 9,037.09
Net Debt		172,617.50
Grand Total		$181,654.59

LIABILITIES

Accounts Owed by District:		
Granite State Fire Alarm	$ 405.00	
Notes and Bonds Outstanding	172,700.00	
Building Fund, 2-Rm Add.	8,549.59	
Total Liabilities		$181,654.59
Grand Total		$181,654.59

STATUS OF SCHOOL NOTES AND BONDS

	Elementary School	2-Room Addition	Total
Outstanding at Beginning of Year	$136,700.00	None	$136,700.00
Issued During year	None	$45,000.00	45,000.00
Total	136,700.00	45,000.00	181,700.00
Payments of Principal of Debt	9,000.00	None	9,000.00
Notes and Bonds Outstanding at End of Year	$127,700.00	$45,000.00	$172,700.00

D. SALARY OF SUPERINTENDENT
July 1, 1959 — June 30, 1960

Paid by:	Per Cent	Salary
Alton School District	19.8	$ 1,138.50
Barnstead School District	6.7	385.25
New Durham School District	4.3	247.25
Pittsfield School District	25.9	1,489.25
Tuftonboro School District	10.6	609.50
Wolfeboro School District	32.7	1,880.25
Total Districts' Share		$ 5,750.00
State of New Hampshire's share from Per Capita Tax		$ 2,500.00

E. ALTON SCHOOL DISTRICT BUDGET
1961-1962

Expenditures—Item	Total Expenditures 1959-60	Budget 1960-1961	Actual Expenditures July 1 to Dec. 31, 1960	School Board's Budget 1961-1962	Budget Committee's Budget 1961-1962
ADMINISTRATION					
Salaries of district officers	$ 464.00	$ 450.00	$ 428.00	$ 0.00	$ 700.00
Superintendent's salary (local share)	1,138.50	1,200.00	1,243.75	1,404.00	1,404.00
Tax for state wide supervision	530.00	522.00	522.00	544.00	544.00
Salaries of other administrative personnel	1,592.66	2,283.00	2,276.70	2,175.00	2,175.00
Supplies and expenses	1,050.39	1,065.00	885	1,099.00	1,099.00
INSTRUCTION					
High school teachers' and principal's salaries	29,884.29	32,910.00	9,076.18	25,930.00	25,930.00
Elementary and principals' salaries	30,642.47	31,740.00	13,219.69	44,420.00	44,420.00
Books and other instruction aids, high	810	880.00	688.95	960.00	960.00
Books and other instruction aids, elementary	447.22	800.00	908.03	706.00	706.00
Scholars' supplies, high	2,129.43	1,400.00	1,266.09	1,950.00	1,950.00
Scholars' supplies, elementary	1,611.09	1,600.00	1,234.25	1,650.00	1,650.00
Salaries of clerical aids, high		200.00	95.50	500.00	500.00
Salaries of clerical aids, elementary		300.00	100.00	220.00	220.00
Supplies and other expenses, high	684.56	800.00	578.48	482.00	482.00
Supplies and other expenses, elementary	421.75	300.00	842.62	600.00	600.00
OPERATION OF SCHOOL PLANT					
Salaries of custodians, high	2,486.19	3,130.00	1,662.21	2,115.00	2,115.00
Salaries of custodians, elementary	3,774.29	3,370.00	1,552.96	4,535.00	4,535.00
Fuel or heat, high	1,804.31	1,600.00	904.55	1,800.00	1,800.00
Fuel or heat, elementary	2,290.76	2,400.00	111.69	2,300.00	2,300.00
Water, light, supplies and gas, high	1,642.61	1,000.00	1,261.76	1,650.00	1,650.00
Water, light, supplies & gas, elementary	1,251.79	1,650.00	524.82	1,325.00	1,325.00

MAINTENANCE OF SCHOOL PLANT

Repairs and ...s, high	663.29	1,500.00	549.63	1,400.00	1,400.00
Repairs and replacements, ...mentary	844.07	1,000.00	1,273.88	1,150.00	1,150.00

AUXILIARY ACTIVITIES

Health ... ...igh	485.98	500.00	133.20	600.00	600.00
Health ... ...ay	999.50	1,050.00	336.00	1,150.00	1,150.00
..., ...ay	12,573.70	13,000.00	5,068.00	13,870.00	13,870.00
Special ...aries and special u...fds, high	1,002.14		600.00	1,465.00	1,465.00
Special ...aries ard special f...ls, ...ay	5.00	650.00	646.40	650.00	650.00
...ool lunch and special milk, high	354.26		75.88		
School ... and special ...id, elementary	788.74		177.05		

FIXED CHARGES

Retirement ard ...ity, high	2,164.03	2,500.00	1,041.99	1,760.00	1,760.00
Retirement ard ...al security, ...ary	2,195.91	2,400.00	551.23	3,569.00	3,569.00
...re, ta...s. ...s and ... ...ps, ...igh	593.98	1,200.00	1,742.49	800.00	800.00
Insurance, ta...s. ...r's and ... ...ps, ...n.	701.16	800.00		990.00	990.00

CONTINGENCY FUND

		1,500.00		3,000.00	3,000.00

...L OUTLAY

Lands and ... ...bs, elementary	568.87	100.00		1,500.00	
...ins and improvements, high	33,?74.98	400.00		200.00	200.00
Additions and ... ...ps, ...ay		100.00			
N...w ... ...nt, high	2,773.61	1,200.00	1,243.04	1,500.00	1,500.00
N...w ... ...nt, elementary	3,698.93	500.00	186.91	1,000.00	1,000.00
...AL CAPITAL OUTLAY	40,806.39	2,300.00	1,429.95	4,200.00	2,700.00

DEBT AND INTEREST

Item	Total Receipts 1959-1960	Amended Budget 1960-1961	Actual Receipts July 1 to Dec. 31, 1960	School Board's Budget 1961-1962	Budget Committee's Budget 1961-1962
Principal of debt	9,000.00	12,000.00	12,000.00	12,000.00	12,000.00
Interest on debt	3,927.24	4,500.00	2,303.93	4,182.25	4,182.25
TOTAL DEBT AND IN REST	12,927.24	16,500.00	14,303.93	16,182.25	16,182.25
TOTAL EXPENDITURES OR SCHOOL APPROPRIATION	$161,786.80	$134,500.00	$67,291.71	$147,851.25	$146,351.25
Receipts—Item					
Balance (actual or est.)	$ 112.71	$ 270.00	$ 252.97		
State aid	2,700.00	3,240.00	3,355.90	3,600.00	3,600.00
Federal Aid	1,748.38	500.00	565.44	300.00	300.00
Building Fund Bal ace					6,254.51
High School tuition	6,674.86	6,255.00		8,244.00	8,244.00
Elementary school tuition	7,689.53	10,175.00		8,618.00	(300
Bond or Note Issues	45,000.00				
Other	266.00	1,500.00	27.80	3,000.00	3,000.00
TOTAL RECEIPTS OTHER THAN PROPERTY TAXES	$ 64,191.48	$ 21,940.00	$ 4,202.11	$ 23,762.00	$ 30,016.51
DISTRICT ASSESSMENT RAISED OR TO BE RAISED BY PROPERTY TAXES	106,397.88	112,560.00	72,560.00	124,089.25	116,334.74
TOTAL APPROPRIATION VOTED BY SCHOOL DISTRICT	$170,589.36	$134,500.00	$76,762.11	$147,851.25	$146,351.25

BUDGET COMMITTEE

GEORGE L. SHAW   A. RAYMOND WHIPPLE

RICHARD S. DOWNING

KENNETH CHASE   ARCHIE A. HORNE

HAROLD A. CLOUGH   JUDSON DOWNING

CHARLES J. BEAUDETTE

OLIVER W. A N E

ROBERT E. JONES

F. SCHOOL LUNCH PROGRAM

FINANCIAL STATEMENT
July 1, 1959 to June 30, 1960

Beginning Balance, July 1, 1959		$ 243.16
Receipts:		
Lunch Sales, Children	$3,709.96	
Lunch Sales, Adults	344.75	
Reimbursement	868.35	
District Appropriation	240.00	
Miscellaneous Cash	153.37	
Total Receipts		$5,316.43
Total available		$5,559.59
Expenditures:		
Food	$4,038.21	
Labor	1,366.72	
Equipment	44.81	
All Other Expenditures	43.30	
Total Expenditures		$5,493.04
Balance, June 30, 1960		$ 66.55

BALANCE SHEET
Fiscal Year Ended June 30, 1960

Assets:		
Cash in Bank	$ 66.55	
Accounts Receivable—		
Reimbursement due Program	218.45	
Food Inventory, June 30	92.53	
Total Assets		$ 377.53

Liabilities:
Withholding Tax Payable $ 133.02
                                   _____

            Total Liabilities $ 133.02
Working Capital   244.51
                                                 _____

        Total Liabilities and Working
            Capital $ 377.53
                            MATTHEW J. FLAHERTY
June 1, 1960

IV REPORTS

A. REPORT OF THE HIGH SCHOOL PRINCIPAL

We have completed our fourth year of testing, using a program that can compare the growth of each pupil, class and total school population, grades 3 through 8, from year to year. The norms used are national age norms and the tests are the Iowa Basic Skills Tests. Our total school percentile for the last four years is as follows:

1958	1959	1960	1961
56%	54%	59%	65.1%

NOTE:—The national average for a school percentile would be 50. Because the tests are diagnostic, our weaknesses can be discovered and then corrective measures taken. We have been pursuing our weak areas and are proud of our progress.

A Post Graduate Picture of Four Classes

	1957	1958	1859	1960
Four Year College	1	3	5	1
Technical School and Other Schooling	2		3	2
Junior Colleges	2	2	3	1
Nursing	1		1	2
Working	6	2	7	6
Married	2	2	4	
Service	2	7	3	3
Unknown			2	2
	16	16	28	17

NOTE:

1. A number of individuals in the service are attending or have attended Service Schools—others are pursuing College Extension Courses.

2. A number of individuals working are earning money to attend college.

Our curriculum has changed with the demands of the times. This year we have added French offerings in grades 5, 7 and 8; total French offerings this year include grades 4, 5, 7, 8, 9, 10, 11 and 12. Next year we plan to add French in grade 6 so as to complete an eight-year continuous program.

Other additions to our program include Social Living—a Sociology course for Seniors; General Business —a course in business arithmetic; Shop Math for the industrial arts program; Arts and Crafts for grades 7-12 pupils and a Band for beginners, grades 4, 5 and 6. Our Physics program was greatly strengthened by Dr. White's Physics Films which we have been using daily throughout the school year.

The Principal was put on a twelve months' basis during the summer of 1960 and, as a result, school opening was smoother.

Mrs. Ann Pearson resigned as Hot Lunch Supervisor. Mrs. Kenneth D. Chase assumed the responsibilities. School lunch servings to pupils so far this year have averaged over 150 daily — about one-half the pupils eat daily hot lunches.

Respectfully submitted,

MATTHEW J. FLAHERTY
Principal, Alton Central School

B. ANNUAL SCHOOL HEALTH SERVICE REPORT

For Year 1960

Number of pupils examined	134
Number of Vision Tests	299
Number of Hearing Tests	299
Number of Inspections	800
Number for Height	299
Number for Weight	299
Number of Urine Specimens Collected	134
Number successfully vaccinated	29
Number of Chicken Pox Cases	1
Number of Mumps Cases	1
Number of Pediculosis Cases	9
Number of Impetigo Cases	5
Number of Defects Found in Ears	2
Number of T & A Cases	2
Number with Defective Teeth	10
Number of Defects Found by School Nurse-Teacher:	
Vision	5
Hearing	2
Skin	4
Posture	35
Speech	1

Teeth	20

Clinics and Special Referrals:
Pre-school Clinic, April, 1960—

Children registered	19
Urine Specimens collected	19
Well Child Conference, children to optometrist	4
Number of Home Visits	50

Examining Physician, O. E. Appleyard, M. D.
June 17, 1960

JEANNE C. PERKINS, R.N.
School Nurse-Teacher

JASON E. BOYNTON
Superintendent of Schools

V WARRANT

TENTATIVE SCHOOL DISTRICT WARRANT
The State of New Hampshire

To the Inhabitants of the School District in the Town
of Alton, New Hampshire, qualified to vote in district affairs:

You are hereby notified to meet at the Memorial
School Auditorium in said district on the eighteenth
day of March, 1961, at two o'clock in the afternoon, to
act upon the following subjects:

1. To choose a Moderator for the coming year.

2. To choose a Clerk for the ensuing year.

3. To choose a Member of the School Board for the
ensuing three years.

4. To choose a Treasurer for the ensuing year.

5. To determine and appoint the salaries of the
School Board and Truant Officer, and fix the compensa-
tion of any other officers or agent of the district.

6. To hear the reports of Agents, Auditors, Committees, or Officers chosen, and pass any vote relating
thereto.

7. To choose Agents, Auditors and Committees in
relation to any subject embraced in this warrant.

8. To see what sum of money the district will raise
and appropriate for the support of schools, for the
salaries of school district officials and agents, and for
the payment of statutory obligations of the district,

and to authorize the application against said appropriation of such sums as are estimated to be received from the state foundation aid fund together with other income; the school board to certify to the selectmen the balance between the estimated revenue and the appropriation, which balance is to be raised by taxes by the town.

9. To transact any other business that may legally come before said meeting.

Given under our hands at said Alton this fourteenth day of February, 1961.

JUDSON DOWNING, Chairman
GLADYS HOWE
HERBERT CARD

School Board

A true copy of Warrant—Attest:
JUDSON DOWNING, Chairman
GLADYS HOWE
HERBERT CARD

School Board

VI SCHOOL CALENDAR

SUPERVISORY SCHOOL UNION NO. 49

1961 - 1962

1961

September	5	General Teachers' Meeting
September	6	Schools Open
October	12	Columbus Day—Schools Closed
October	20	Teachers' Convention—Schools Closed
November	22	Thanksgiving Recess—Schools Close 1 p.m.
November	27	Schools Open
December	22	Christmas Vacation—Schools Close 3 p.m.

1962

January	2	Schools Open
February	16	Winter Vacation—Schools Close 3 p.m.
February	26	Schools Open
March	30	Good Friday—Schools Close 1 p.m.
April	20	Spring Vacation—Schools Close 3 p.m.
April	30	Schools Open
May	30	Memorial Day—Schools Closed
June	19	Summer Vacation—Schools Close 1 p.m.

SCHOOL DAYS EACH MONTH

September	18	February	15
October	20	March	21½
November	20	April	16
December	16	May	22
January	22 (1962)	June	12½
	Total Days,	183	

This calendar has been designed to comply with RSA 189:1 as amended by the 1959 General Court and the Statement of Policy approved by the State Board of Education in March of 1960. Teachers' attendance at the State Teachers' Convention will not count as a school day.

This calendar is subject to changes authorized by the School Board, State of New Hampshire education authorities, or when school is called off because of dangerous storms and emergencies. The minimum legal requirement of 180 days might necessitate continuing beyond June 19 if more than three school days are lost.